HOUGHTON MIFFLIN HARCOURT

MATH
Expressions
Common Core

Dr. Karen C. Fuson

GRADE

3

Volume 2

This material is based upon work supported by the
National Science Foundation
under Grant Numbers
ESI-9816320, REC-9806020, and RED-935373.

Any opinions, findings, and conclusions, or recommendations expressed in this material
are those of the author and do not necessarily reflect the views of the National Science Foundation.

HOUGHTON MIFFLIN HARCOURT

Printed in the U.S.A.

ISBN: 978-0-547-82440-6

7 8 9 10 0868 21 20 19 18 17 16 15 14

4500478331   A B C D E F G

VOLUME 2 CONTENTS

UNIT 4 Multidigit Addition and Subtraction

© Houghton Mifflin Harcourt Publishing Company

BIG IDEA 3	Ungroup to Subtract

UNIT 5 Write Equations to Solve Word Problems

BIG IDEA 1	Types of Word Problems

BIG IDEA 2	Solve Two Step Word Problems

UNIT 6 Polygons, Perimeter, and Area

BIG IDEA 1   Analyzing Triangles and Quadrilaterals

BIG IDEA 2   Area and Perimeter

UNIT 7 Explore Fractions

STUDENT RESOURCES

Dear Family,

Your child is currently participating in math activities that help him or her to understand place value, rounding, and addition and subtraction of 3-digit numbers.

- **Place Value Drawings:** Students learn to represent numbers with drawings that show how many hundreds, tens, and ones are in the numbers. Hundreds are represented by boxes. Tens are represented by vertical line segments, called ten sticks. Ones are represented by small circles. The drawings are also used to help students understand regrouping in addition and subtraction. Here is a place value drawing for the number 178.

1 hundred   7 tens   8 ones

Share with your family the Family Letter on Activity Workbook pages 149–150.

The 7 ten sticks and 8 circles are grouped in 5s so students can see the quantities easily and avoid errors.

- **Secret Code Cards:** Secret Code Cards are a set of cards for hundreds, tens, and ones. Students learn about place value by assembling the cards to show two- and three-digit numbers. Here is how the number 148 would be assembled.

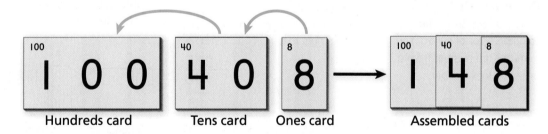

Hundreds card   Tens card   Ones card   Assembled cards

Estimate Sums and Differences Students learn to estimate sums and differences by rounding numbers. They also use estimates to check that their actual answers are reasonable.

	Rounded to the nearest hundred	Rounded to the nearest ten
493	500	490
129	100	130
+ 369	+ 400	+ 370
991	Estimate: 1,000	Estimate: 990

Addition Methods: Students may use the common U.S. method, referred to as the New Groups Above Method, as well as two alternative methods. In the New Groups Below Method, students add from right to left and write the new ten and new hundred on the line. In the Show All Totals method, students add in either direction, write partial sums and then add the partial sums to get the total. Students also use proof drawings to demonstrate grouping 10 ones to make a new ten and grouping 10 tens to make a new hundred.

The New Groups Below Method shows the teen number 13 better than does the New Groups Above Method, where the 1 and 3 are separated. Also, addition is easier in New Groups Below, where you add the two numbers you see and just add 1.

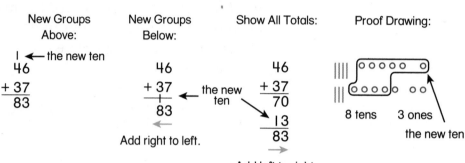

New Groups Above:

```
 1 ← the new ten
 46
+37
 83
```

New Groups Below:

```
  46
+ 37
    1
  83
```
← the new ten

Add right to left.

Show All Totals:

```
  46
+ 37
  70
  13
  83
```

Add left to right.

Proof Drawing:

8 tens   3 ones

the new ten

Subtraction Methods: Students may use the common U.S. method in which the subtraction is done right to left, with the ungrouping done before each column is subtracted. They also learn an alternative method in which all the ungrouping is done *before* the subtracting. If they do all the ungrouping first, students can subtract either from left to right or from right to left.

The Ungroup First Method helps students avoid the common error of subtracting a smaller top number from a larger bottom number.

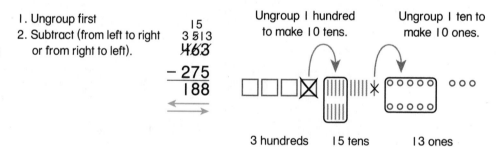

1. Ungroup first
2. Subtract (from left to right or from right to left).

```
       15
   3 5 13
   4̶6̶3̶
 - 2 7 5
   1 8 8
```

Ungroup 1 hundred to make 10 tens.

Ungroup 1 ten to make 10 ones.

3 hundreds   15 tens   13 ones

Please call if you have any questions or comments.

Thank you.

Sincerely,
Your child's teacher

COMMON CORE

This unit includes the Common Core Standards for Mathematical Content for Operations and Algebraic Thinking, 3.OA.8; Number and Operation in Base Ten, 3.NBT.1 and 3.NBT.2 and all Mathematical Practices.

Make Place Value Drawings

Estimada familia:

Su niño está participando en actividades matemáticas que le servirán para comprender el valor posicional, el redondeo y la suma y resta de números de 3 dígitos.

- **Dibujos de valor posicional:** Los estudiantes aprenden a representar números por medio de dibujos que muestran cuántas centenas, decenas y unidades contienen. Las centenas están representadas con casillas, las decenas con segmentos verticales, llamados palitos de decenas, y las unidades con círculos pequeños. Los dibujos también se usan para ayudar a los estudiantes a comprender cómo se reagrupa en la suma y en la resta. Este es un dibujo de valor posicional para el número 178.

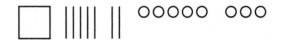

1 centena   7 decenas   8 unidades

Muestra a tu familia la Carta a la familia de las páginas 151 y 152 del Cuaderno de actividades y trabajo.

Los palitos de decenas y los círculos se agrupan en grupos de 5 para que las cantidades se puedan ver más fácilmente y se eviten errores.

- **Tarjetas de código secreto:** Las tarjetas de código secreto son un conjunto de tarjetas con centenas, decenas y unidades. Los estudiantes aprenden acerca del valor posicional organizando las tarjetas de manera que muestren números de dos y de tres dígitos. Así se puede formar el número 148:

Tarjeta de centenas   Tarjeta de decenas   Tarjeta de unidades   Tarjetas organizadas

Estimar sumas y diferencias: Los estudiantes aprenden a estimar sumas y diferencias redondeando números. También usan las estimaciones para comprobar que sus respuestas son razonables.

	Redondear a la centena más próxima	Redondear a la decena más próxima
493	500	490
129	100	130
+ 369	+ 400	+ 370
991	Estimación: 1,000	Estimación: 990

Métodos de suma: Los estudiantes pueden usar el método común de EE. UU., conocido como Grupos nuevos arriba, y otros dos métodos alternativos. En el método de Grupos nuevos abajo, los estudiantes suman de derecha a izquierda y escriben la nueva decena y la nueva centena en el renglón. En el método de Mostrar todos los totales, los estudiantes suman en cualquier dirección, escriben sumas parciales y luego las suman para obtener el total. Los estudiantes también usan dibujos de comprobación para demostrar cómo se agrupan 10 unidades para formar una nueva decena, y 10 decenas para formar una nueva centena.

El método de Grupos nuevos abajo muestra el número 13 mejor que el método de Grupos nuevos arriba, en el que se separan los números 1 y 3. Además, es más fácil sumar con Grupos nuevos abajo, donde se suman los dos números que se ven y simplemente se añade 1.

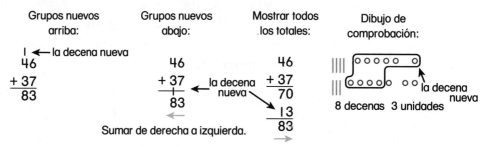

Grupos nuevos arriba:

1 ← la decena nueva
46
+ 37
83

Grupos nuevos abajo:

46
+ 37
83

Sumar de derecha a izquierda.

Mostrar todos los totales:

46
+ 37
70
13
83

Sumar de izquierda a derecha.

Dibujo de comprobación:

8 decenas 3 unidades la decena nueva

Métodos de resta: Los estudiantes pueden usar el método común de EE. UU., en el cual la resta se hace de derecha a izquierda, desagrupando antes de restar cada columna. También aprenden un método alternativo en el que desagrupan todo *antes* de restar. Si los estudiantes desagrupan todo primero, pueden restar de izquierda a derecha o de derecha a izquierda.

El método de Desagrupar primero ayuda a los estudiantes a evitar el error común de restar un número pequeño de arriba, de un número más grande de abajo.

1. Desagrupar primero.
2. Restar (de izquierda a derecha o de derecha a izquierda).

15
3 5̶ 13
4̶6̶3̶
− 275
188

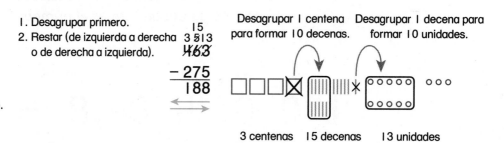

Desagrupar 1 centena para formar 10 decenas.

Desagrupar 1 decena para formar 10 unidades.

3 centenas   15 decenas   13 unidades

Si tiene alguna pregunta o algún comentario, por favor comuníquese conmigo. Gracias.

Atentamente,
El maestro de su niño

COMMON CORE Esta unidad incluye los Common Core Standards for Mathematical Content for Operations and Algebraic Thinking, 3.OA.8; Number and Operation in Base Ten, 3.NBT.1 and 3.NBT.2 and all Mathematical Practices.

▶ Practice Place Value Drawings to 999

Write the number for each dot drawing.

1.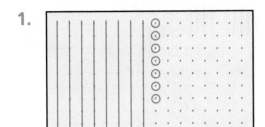

2.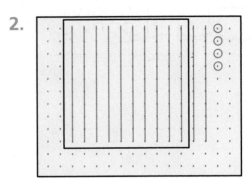

Write the number for each place value drawing.

3. ☐ ☐ ||||| || ○○○○○ ○○

4. ☐ ☐ ☐ ||||| | ○

5. ☐ ☐ ☐ || ○○○
   ☐ ☐ ☐

6. ☐ ☐ ☐ |||| ○○○○○ ○○○○
   ☐

Make a place value drawing for each number.

7. 86

8. 587

4-1
Class Activity

► Practice with the Thousand Model

Write the number for each place value drawing.

9. 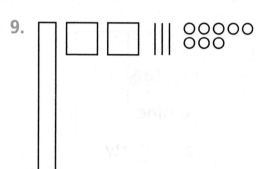   10.

Make a place value drawing for each number.

11. 2,368

12. 5,017

► Write Numbers for Word Names

Write the number for the words.

13. eighty-two

14. ninety-nine

15. four hundred sixty-seven

16. nine hundred six

17. one thousand, fifteen

18. eight thousand, one hundred twenty

Make Place Value Drawings

▶ Read and Write Numbers

Write the number for the words.

1. two hundred twelve

2. two thousand, eight

3. nine hundred ninety-one

4. six thousand, fifty-one

5. four hundred sixteen

6. six hundred nine

7. nine hundred eighty-seven

8. five thousand, thirty

9. four thousand, seventeen

10. eight thousand, six hundred

Write the word name for each number.

11. 783

12. 907

13. 3,001

14. 8,043

Write each number in expanded form.

15. 314

16. 2,148

17. 7,089

18. 8,305

Write each number in standard form.

19. 5 thousands + 8 tens + 7 ones

20. 6 thousands + 4 hundreds + 5 ones

► Solve and Discuss

Use a place value drawing to help you solve each problem. Label your answers.

21. Scott baked a batch of rolls. He gave a bag of 10 rolls to each of 7 friends. He kept 1 roll for himself. How many rolls did he bake in all?

22. Sixty-two bags of hot dog buns were delivered to the school cafeteria. Each bag had 10 buns. How many buns were delivered?

Mario and Rosa baked 89 corn muffins.
They put the muffins in boxes of 10.

---

23. How many boxes did they fill?

24. How many muffins were left over?

Zoe's scout troop collected 743 cans of food to donate to a shelter. They put the cans in boxes of 10.

---

25. How many boxes did they fill?

26. How many cans were left over?

27. **Math Journal** Write your own place value word problem. Make a drawing to show how to solve your problem.

VOCABULARY
hundreds
tens
ones

▶ Scrambled Place Value Names

Unscramble the place values and write the number.

1. 8 **ones** + 6 **hundreds** + 4 **tens**

2. 9 hundreds + 7 tens + 1 one

3. 5 ones + 0 tens + 7 hundreds

4. 5 tens + 4 ones + 3 hundreds

5. 2 tens + 2 hundreds + 2 ones

6. 8 hundreds + 3 ones + 6 tens

Unscramble the place values and write the number.
Then, make a place value drawing for the number.

7. 6 hundreds + 9 ones + 3 tens

8. 9 ones + 3 tens + 8 hundreds

9. 8 ones + 3 hundreds + 4 tens

10. 2 hundreds + 9 tens + 1 one

▶ Solve and Discuss

Solve each problem. Label your answer.

11. The bookstore received 35 boxes of books. Each box held 10 books. How many books did the store receive?

> Maya's family picked 376 apples and put them in baskets. Each basket held 10 apples.

12. How many baskets did they fill?   13. How many apples were left over?

> Aidee had 672 buttons. She put them in bags of 100 buttons each.

14. How many bags did Aidee fill?   15. How many buttons were left over?

> When Joseph broke open his piggy bank, there were 543 pennies inside. He grouped the pennies into piles of 100.

16. How many piles of 100 did Joseph make?   17. How many extra pennies did he have?

▶ Estimate

Solve the problem.

1. Tasha read three books over the summer. Here is the number of pages in each book:

Watership Down	494 pages
Sounder	128 pages
The Secret Garden	368 pages

About how many pages did Tasha read? Explain how you made your **estimate.**

▶ Practice Rounding

Round each number to the nearest hundred. Use drawings or Secret Code Cards if they help you.

2. 128   3. 271   4. 376

5. 649   6. 415   7. 550

8. 62   9. 1,481   10. 2,615

11. **Explain Your Thinking** When you round a number to the nearest hundred, how do you know whether to round up or round down?

Show your work on your paper or in your journal.

▶ Solve Problems by Estimating

Solve by rounding to the nearest hundred.

12. At the Lakeside School, there are 286 second graders, 341 third graders, and 377 fourth graders. About how many students are there at the Lakeside School?

13. Last week, Mrs. Larson drove 191 miles on Monday, 225 miles on Wednesday, and 107 miles on Friday. About how many miles did she drive altogether?

14. Of the 832 people at the hockey game, 292 sat on the visiting team side. The rest sat on the home team side. About how many people sat on the home team side?

▶ Reasonable Answers

**Use rounding to decide if the answer is reasonable.
Then find the answer to see if you were right.**

15. $604 - 180 = 586$

16. $377 + 191 = 568$

17. $268 - 17 = 107$

18. $1{,}041 + 395 = 646$

19. $407 - 379 = 28$

20. $535 + 287 = 642$

▶ Round 2-Digit Numbers to the Nearest Ten

Round each number to the nearest ten.

1. 63

2. 34

3. 78

4. 25

5. 57

6. 89

7. 42

8. 92

▶ Round 3-Digit Numbers to the Nearest Ten

Round each number to the nearest ten.

9. 162

10. 741

11. 309

12. 255

13. 118

14. 197

15. 503

16. 246

17. **Explain Your Thinking** When you round a number to the nearest ten, how do you know whether to round up or round down?

▶ Estimate the Answer

Solve each problem.

18. The chart at the right shows how many smoothies the Juice Hut sold yesterday. By rounding each number to the nearest ten, estimate how many smoothies the Juice Hut sold in all.

Smoothies Sold at Juice Hut
13 raspberry-peach smoothies
38 strawberry-banana smoothies
44 guava-mango smoothies
61 peach-blueberry smoothies

19. Ms. Singh has 52 rock CDs, 75 jazz CDs, 36 classical CDs, and 23 hip-hop CDs. Round each number to the nearest ten to find *about* how many CDs she has.

20. Roz rented a video that is 123 minutes long. She watched 48 minutes of it. Round each number to the nearest ten to estimate how many more minutes she has to watch.

Use the table at the right to solve Problems 21–23.

21. Estimate the total number of books the school received by rounding each number to the nearest hundred.

Jefferson Elementary School Books Received	
Math	436
Reading	352

22. Estimate the total number of books the school received by rounding each number to the nearest ten.

23. Find the total number of math and reading books. Which of your estimates is closer to the actual total?

▶ **Reasonable Answers**

**Use rounding to decide if the answer is reasonable.
Write *yes* or *no*. Then find the answer to see if you
were correct.**

24. 93 − 29 = 64   25. 113 + 57 = 140   26. 83 + 19 = 102

27. 336 + 258 = 594   28. 438 − 158 = 280   29. 437 + 199 = 536

30. 725 − 235 = 590   31. 249 + 573 = 822   32. 542 − 167 = 475

▶ What's the Error?

Dear Math Students,

Today my teacher asked me to estimate the answer to this problem:

Ms. Smith's class brought in 384 soup labels. Mr. Alvarez's class brought in 524 soup labels. About how many labels did the two classes bring in?

$$384 \longrightarrow 300$$
$$+524 \longrightarrow \underline{+500}$$
$$800$$

About 800 soup labels were brought in.

Is my answer correct? If not, please correct my work and tell me what I did wrong.

Your friend,
Puzzled Penguin

33. Write an answer to Puzzled Penguin.

▶ Estimate the Number of Objects

Jar D has 100 Beans. Estimate how many beans are in the other jars.

34. Jar A

35. Jar B

36. Jar C

► Solve and Discuss

Solve each problem. Label your answer. Use your Mathboard or a separate sheet of paper.

1. Elena made necklaces for her friends. She used 586 green beads and 349 red beads. How many beads did Elena use in all?

2. Fabrice has a collection of 485 basketball cards and 217 baseball cards. How many sports cards does Fabrice have in all?

► PATH to FLUENCY **Introduce Addition Methods**

Tonya and Mark collect seashells. Tonya has 249 shells, and Mark has 386 shells. How many shells do they have in all?

Here are three ways to find the answer:

Show All Totals Method	New Groups Below Method	New Groups Above Method
249 + 386 ──── 500 120 + 15 ──── 635	249 + 386 ──── 635	$\overset{1\ 1}{249}$ + 386 ──── 635

Proof Drawing:

6 hundreds   3 tens   5 ones

▶ PATH to FLUENCY **Practice Addition Methods**

Solve each problem. Make proof drawings to show that your answers are correct.

3. Ryan has two stamp albums. One album has 554 stamps, and the other has 428 stamps. How many stamps does Ryan have in all?

4. One week Ashley read 269 pages. The next week she read 236 pages. What is the total number of pages she read in the two weeks?

5. The video store has 445 comedy videos and 615 drama videos. How many comedy and drama videos does the store have altogether?

6. Ali has 128 photos of her pets and 255 photos of her family. How many photos does Ali have altogether?

Explore Multidigit Addition

Show your work on your paper or in your journal.

► **PATH to FLUENCY** **Solve and Discuss**

Solve each problem using a numerical method and a proof drawing.

1. There are 359 cars and 245 trucks in the parking garage. How many vehicles are in the garage?

2. The Creepy Crawler exhibit at the science museum has 693 spiders and 292 centipedes. How many spiders and centipedes are there in all?

3. On Saturday, 590 people went to the art museum. On Sunday, 355 went to the museum. How many people went to the museum altogether?

4. There were 120 people on the ferry yesterday. Today the ferry had 767 people. How many people in all were on the ferry during the past two days?

▶ What's the Error?

Dear Math Students,

Today I found the answer to 168 + 78, but I don't know if I added correctly. Please look at my work. Is my answer right? If not, please correct my work and tell what I did wrong.

Your friend,
Puzzled Penguin

$$\begin{array}{r} 168 \\ +78 \\ \hline 948 \end{array}$$

5. Write an answer to Puzzled Penguin.

▶ PATH to FLUENCY Line Up the Places to Add

Write each addition vertically. Line up the places correctly. Then add and make a proof drawing.

6. 179 + 38 = ▮

7. 650 + 345 = ▮

8. 407 + 577 = ▮

► (PATH to FLUENCY) **Decide When to Group**

**Decide which new groups you will make.
Then add to see if you were correct.**

1. 123	2. 358	3. 732	4. 416
+ 247	+ 434	+ 189	+ 396

Add.

5. 647	6. 132	7. 554	8. 168
+ 178	+ 763	+ 257	+ 692

9. 384	10. 631	11. 464	12. 313
+ 586	+ 189	+ 446	+ 649

13. 576 + 265   14. 389 + 511   15. 568 + 219   16. 137 + 284

Write an equation and solve the problem.

17. The first animated film at the movie theatre
lasted 129 minutes. The second film lasted
104 minutes. How many minutes in all did
the two movies last?

▶ Solve and Discuss

Write an equation and solve the problem.

18. Jacob has 347 basketball cards in his collection. He has 256 baseball cards. How many cards does he have altogether?

19. Jasmine's family drove for two days to visit her grandparents. They drove 418 miles on the first day and 486 miles on the second day. How many miles did they drive in all?

20. The florist ordered 398 roses and 562 tulips. How many flowers did the florist order in all?

21. Emilio checked a suitcase at the airport. His suitcase weighed 80 pounds. His wife checked three suitcases. Each of her suitcases weighed 30 pounds. How many pounds in all did their suitcases weigh?

22. Write and solve an addition word problem where 287 and 614 are addends.

▶ Add Three-Digit Numbers

School Carnival Rides

Rides	Tickets Sold
Twister	298
Monster Mix	229
Crazy Coaster	193
Mega Wheel	295
Bumper Cars	301

Write an equation and solve the problem.

1. How many people went on the two most popular rides?

Show your work on your paper or in your journal.

2. The total tickets sold for which two rides was 494?

3. Tickets for the Monster Mix and Crazy Coaster sold for $2. How much money did the school earn on the ticket sales for these two rides?

4. About how many tickets were sold for Twister, Monster Mix, and Mega Wheel altogether?

5. The total tickets sold for which three rides equals about 900?

► Use Addition to Solve Problems

Student Collections

Type of Collection	Number of Objects
rocks	403
stamps	371
shells	198
buttons	562
miniature cars	245

Write an equation and solve the problem.

6. How many objects are in the two smallest collections?

Show your work on your paper or in your journal.

7. The total number of objects in two collections is 760. What are the collections?

8. Are the combined collections of shells and buttons greater than or less than the combined collections of rocks and stamps?

9. Is the estimated sum of stamps, shells, and miniature cars closer to 700 or to 800?

10. Suppose another student has a collection of sports cards. The number of sports cards is 154 greater than the number of rocks. How many cards are in the sports cards collection?

Practice Addition

Show your work on your paper or in your journal.

► (**PATH to FLUENCY**) **Discuss Subtraction Methods**

Solve this word problem.

> Mr. Kim had 134 jazz CDs. He sold 58 of them at his garage sale. How many jazz CDs does he have now?

1. Write a subtraction that you could do to answer this question.

2. Make a place value drawing for 134. Take away 58. How many are left?

3. Write a numerical solution method for what you did in the drawing.

4. Describe how you ungrouped to subtract.

VOCABULARY
ungrouping
subtract

▶ What's the Error?

Dear Math Students,

Today I found the answer to 134 – 58, but I don't know if I did it correctly. Please look at my work. Is my answer right? If not, please correct my work and tell what I did wrong.

```
 134
- 58
─────
 124
```

Your friend,
Puzzled Penguin

5. Write an answer to Puzzled Penguin.

Show your work on your paper or in your journal.

▶ (PATH to FLUENCY) Subtraction Detective

To avoid making subtraction mistakes, look at the top number closely. Do all the **ungrouping** you need to *before* you **subtract**. The magnifying glass around the top number helps you remember to be a "subtraction detective."

Subtract. Show your ungroupings numerically and with proof drawings.

6.
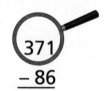
371
− 86

7.

163
− 47

8.

459
−175

9.

277
− 68

Ungroup to Subtract

Show your work on your paper or in your journal.

▶ **PATH to FLUENCY** **Ungroup to Subtract**

Solve each problem. Show your work numerically and with proof drawings.

1. Lakesha bought a box of 500 paper clips. So far, she has used 138 of them. How many are left?

2. A movie theater has 400 seats. At the noon show, 329 seats were filled. How many seats were empty?

3. At the start of the school year, Seiko had a brand new box of 300 crayons. Now 79 crayons are broken. How many unbroken crayons does Seiko have?

Show your work on your paper or in your journal.

▶ **PATH to FLUENCY** **Subtract Across Zeros**

Solve each problem. Show your work numerically and with proof drawings.

4. The students at Freedom Elementary School have a goal of reading 900 books. They have read 342 books. How many books do the students have left to read?

5. There are 500 books in the Freedom Elementary School library. There are 179 fewer non-fiction than fiction books. How many books are fiction?

6. The students at Olympia Elementary School collected 1,000 bottles for recycling. The students at Sterling Elementary collected 768 bottles. How many more bottles did the students at Olympia collect?

▶ PATH to FLUENCY **Practice Subtracting Across Zeros**

Subtract. Make proof drawings for Exercises 7–10 on MathBoards or on a separate sheet of paper.

7. 8 0 0
    − 3 9 1

8. 5 0 0
    − 3 3 3

9. 4 0 0
    − 2 1 7

10. 9 0 0
     − 8 1 8

11. 6 0 0
     − 5 7 5

12. 7 0 0
     − 2 4 8

13. 2 0 0
     − 1 0 9

14. 8 0 0
     − 5 1 9

15. Math Journal Write a word problem that is solved by subtracting a 2-digit number from a 3-digit number that has a zero in both the ones and tens places. Then solve the problem.

► PATH to FLUENCY **Practice Deciding When to Ungroup**

Subtract. Make proof drawings if you need to on MathBoards or on a separate sheet of paper.

16. 912 − 265

17. 323 − 147

18. 280 − 136

19. 489 − 263

20.   754
    − 389

21.   912
    − 437

22.   341
    − 178

23.   603
    − 464

Subtract Across Zeros

► PATH to FLUENCY **Ungroup from Left or Right**

Tony and Maria each solved this problem:

On Tuesday morning, a music store had 463 copies of the new School Daze CD. By the end of the day, they had sold 275 copies. How many copies were left?

Tony	Maria
Tony started ungrouping from the left.	Maria started ungrouping from the right.
1. He has enough hundreds.	1. She does not have enough ones. She ungroups 1 ten to make 10 more ones.
2. He does not have enough tens. He ungroups 1 hundred to make 10 more tens. 	
3. He does not have enough ones. He ungroups 1 ten to make 10 more ones. 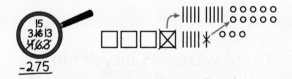	2. She does not have enough tens. She ungroups 1 hundred to get 10 more tens. 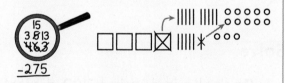
	3. She has enough hundreds.
4. Complete the subtraction. 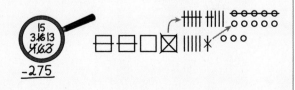	4. Complete the subtraction. 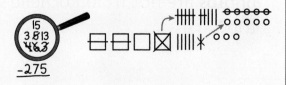

▶ PATH to FLUENCY **Choose a Method to Subtract**

Subtract.

1. 686
    − 387

2. 340
    − 167

3. 765
    − 498

4. 841
    − 253

5. 912
    − 575

6. 853
    − 194

7. 705
    − 429

8. 998
    − 299

9. 513
    − 156

10. 627 − 348

11. 544 − 169

12. 810 − 261

Solve.

13. Rochelle is putting 302 digital photos in an album. Of these, 194 are from her trip to the Grand Canyon. How many photos are not from Rochelle's trip?

14. There were 645 bicycles in a race. Toby finished eighty-seventh. How many bicycles finished after Toby?

► PATH to FLUENCY **Relate Addition and Subtraction**

Solve each problem. Make a proof drawing if you need to.

1. There were 138 students in the gym for the assembly. Then 86 more students came in. How many students were in the gym altogether?

2. There were 224 students in the gym for the assembly. Then 86 students left. How many students were still in the gym?

3. Look at your addition, subtraction, and proof drawings from Problems 1 and 2. How are addition and subtraction related?

Show your work on your paper or in your journal.

▶ Solve and Discuss

Solve. Label your answers.

4. Marly had 275 baseball cards. Her brother gave her a collection of 448 baseball cards. How many baseball cards does Marly have now?

5. Write a subtraction word problem related to the addition word problem in Problem 4. Then find the answer without doing any calculations.

6. Bill drove 375 miles on the first day of his cross-country trip. The next day he drove an additional 528 miles. How many miles did Bill drive on the first two days of his trip?

7. Write a subtraction problem related to the addition word problem in Problem 6. Then find the answer without doing any calculations.

Relate Addition and Subtraction

Show your work on your paper or in your journal.

▶ Subtract and Check

Solve each problem.

1. Ken collects photographs as a hobby. He has 375 photographs in his collection at home. If Ken brought 225 of his photographs to share with his classmates, how many photographs did he leave at home?

2. Of the 212 third- and fourth-grade students, 165 attended the school festival. How many students did not attend the festival?

3. Becky's mom has 653 CDs in her collection. Becky's aunt has 438 CDs in her collection. How many more CDs does Becky's mom have than Becky's aunt?

4. Andrea and John need 750 tickets to get a board game. They have 559 tickets. How many more tickets do they need?

► PATH to FLUENCY **Practice Deciding When to Ungroup**

Answer each question.

Adair subtracted 595 from 834.

---

5. Did she have to ungroup to make more tens? Explain.

6. Did she have to ungroup to make more ones? Explain.

Beatrice subtracted 441 from 950.

---

7. Did she have to ungroup to make more tens? Explain.

8. Did she have to ungroup to make more ones? Explain.

Wan subtracted 236 from 546.

---

9. Did he have to ungroup to make more tens? Explain.

10. Did he have to ungroup to make more ones? Explain.

► (PATH to FLUENCY) **Practice Addition and Subtraction**

Add or subtract.

1. 112
 + 459

2. 572
 − 357

3. 253
 + 328

4. 710
 − 464

5. 461
 − 182

6. 540
 + 175

7. 921
 − 653

8. 398
 − 99

9. 712
 + 189

10. 600
 − 223

11. 809
 − 576

12. 634
 + 287

Solve.

13. The height of Angeline Falls in Washington is 450 feet. Snoqualmie Falls in Washington is 182 feet lower than Angeline Falls. What is the height of Snoqualmie Falls?

14. Jill scored 534 points at the arcade on Friday night. She scored 396 points on Saturday night. How many points did she score altogether?

▶ Solve Real World Problems

The students at Liberty Elementary collected pennies for a fundraiser.

Pennies Collected	
Grade	**Number of Pennies**
Grade 1	225
Grade 2	436
Grade 3	517
Grade 4	609
Grade 5	342

Write an equation and solve the problem.

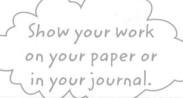

Show your work on your paper or in your journal.

15. How many pennies did Grades 2 and 5 collect?

16. How many more pennies did Grades 1 and 3 collect than Grade 4?

17. Is the total number of pennies collected by Grades 1 and 4 greater than or less than the total number collected by Grades 3 and 5?

18. The total number of pennies collected by which three grades equals about 1,000?

19. Suppose the kindergarten students collected 198 fewer pennies than the Grade 3 students. How many pennies would the kindergarteners have collected?

Addition and Subtraction Practice

▶ Solve Multistep Word Problems

Solve each problem. Label your answers.

1. Isabel bought 36 pieces of fruit for her soccer team. There are 16 apples, 12 bananas, and the rest are pears. How many pieces of fruit are pears?

2. Toby has a collection of sports cards. He had 13 baseball cards, 16 basketball cards, and 14 football cards. Toby sold 15 cards and he bought 17 hockey cards. What is the total number of cards in Toby's collection now?

3. There are 15 more boys than girls in the school band. There are 27 girls. How many students are in the school band?

4. Finn delivered 13 pizzas. Then he delivered 8 more pizzas. Altogether, he delivered 6 fewer pizzas than Liz. How many pizzas did Liz deliver?

5. Majeed built 7 car models and 14 airplane models. Jasmine built 9 more car models than Majeed and 6 fewer airplane models. How many models did Jasmine build in all?

Show your work
on your paper or
in your journal.

► Reasonable Answers

Use rounding to decide if the answer is reasonable. Write
yes **or** *no*. **Then find the answer to see if you were correct.**

6. Nathan counted 28 large dogs and 37 small dogs
   at the dog park. He said he saw 55 dogs in all.

7. There are 122 third-and fourth-grade students at
   Cedar Creek Elementary School. There are 67 students
   in third grade and 55 students in fourth grade.

8. The pet supermarket sold 245 bags of dog food and
   167 bags of cat food. The supermarket sold 312 bags
   of pet food in all.

9. The total distance from Charleston, West Virginia
   to Biloxi, Mississippi is 913 miles. Benjamin drove
   455 miles from Charleston to Athens, Georgia.
   Then he drove 458 miles from Athens to Biloxi.

10. There were 432 people at the basketball game.
    257 people sat on the home team side. 175 people
    sat on the visiting team side.

11. The Pecos River is 234 miles longer than the
    Yellowstone River. The Yellowstone River is
    692 miles long. The Pecos River is 826 miles long.

Solve Word Problems

▶ Math and Maps

The Pony Express was a mail service from St. Joseph, Missouri, to Sacramento, California. The Pony Express service carried mail by horseback riders in relays.

Use the information on the map for Problems 1–3. Write an equation and solve the problem.

Show your work on your paper or in your journal.

1. How many miles did the Pony Express riders travel on a trip from Sacramento to Salt Lake City?

2. The total distance from St. Joseph to Fort Laramie is 616 miles. How many miles is it from Julesburg to Fort Laramie?

3. Write and solve a problem that can be answered using the map.

▶ Use a Table

It took the Pony Express 10 days to deliver letters between Sacramento and St. Joseph. Today we send emails that are delivered within a few minutes. The chart below shows the number of emails sent in a month by different students.

Number of Emails Sent last Month					
Name	Robbie	Samantha	Ellen	Bryce	Callie
Number	528	462	942	388	489

Use the information in the table for Problems 4–6.
Write an equation and solve the problem.

4. How many more emails did Robbie send than Callie?

5. How many more emails did Ellen send than Bryce and Samantha combined?

6. Tamara said that Robbie and Bryce together sent 806 emails. Is her answer reasonable? Explain. Then find the actual answer to see if you are correct.

Focus on Mathematical Practices

UNIT 4
Review/Test

Use the Activity Workbook Unit Test on pages 157–158.

VOCABULARY
estimate
subtract
hundreds
thousands

▶ Vocabulary

Choose the best word from the box.

1. When you _____?_____ 100 from 400, the difference is 300. (Lesson 4-11)

2. The number 732 is equal to 6 _____?_____, 13 tens, and 2 ones. (Lesson 4-1)

3. To find an answer that is close to the exact answer, you can _____?_____. (Lesson 4-5)

▶ Concepts and Skills

4. Make a place value drawing to show how to add 285 and 176. (Lesson 4-7)

```
   285
+  176
```

5. Explain how to estimate the sum of 654 and 142 by rounding to the nearest hundred. (Lessons 4-5, 4-6)

6. Explain where and how to ungroup to do this subtraction. (Lessons 4-11, 4-12)

```
   768
-  575
```

UNIT 4 TEST

255

Add or subtract.

(Lessons 4-1, 4-2, 4-3, 4-4, 4-7, 4-8, 4-9, 4-10, 4-11, 4-12, 4-13, 4-15, 4-16, 4-18)

7.
$$772 \\ + 129$$

8.
$$617 \\ - 549$$

9.
$$457 \\ + 123$$

10.
$$800 \\ - 684$$

11.
$$329 \\ + 598$$

12.
$$831 \\ + 129$$

13.
$$900 \\ - 754$$

14.
$$267 \\ - 125$$

15. $531 - 32 =$

16. $713 + 88 =$

17. $604 - 138 =$

▶ Problem Solving

Solve. (Lessons 4-6, 4-9, 4-10, 4-14, 4-17)

18. Gordon baked 346 blueberry muffins and 287 bran muffins, How many muffins did he bake in all?

19. Write a subtraction word problem related to the addition problem in Problem 18. Then find the answer without doing any calculations.

20. **Extended Response** Veronica has 425 baseball cards. She gave 125 of them to her brother. Veronica's cousin gave her 285 baseball cards. Veronica says she now has 833 baseball cards. Is her answer reasonable? Explain. Then find the actual answer to check if you are correct.

Dear Family,

In this unit, your child will solve addition, subtraction, multiplication, and division problems involving unknown addends and factors.

- If one of the addends is unknown, it can be found by subtracting the known addend from the total or by counting on from the known addend to the total.
- If the total is unknown, it can be found by adding the addends.
- If one of the factors is unknown, it can be found by dividing the product by the other factor.
- If the product is unknown, it can be found by multiplying the factors.

Share with your family the Family Letter on Activity Workbook page 159.

Math Mountains are used to show a total and two addends. Students can use the Math Mountain to write an equation and then solve the equation to find the unknown.

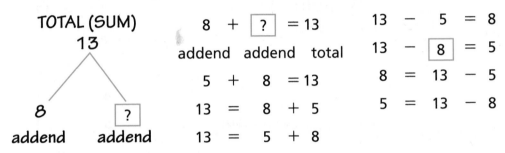

TOTAL (SUM)
13
8   ?
addend   addend

$8 + \boxed{?} = 13$
addend addend total

$5 + 8 = 13$

$13 = 8 + 5$

$13 = 5 + 8$

$13 - 5 = 8$

$13 - \boxed{8} = 5$

$8 = 13 - 5$

$5 = 13 - 8$

Equations with numbers alone on the left are also emphasized to help with the understanding of algebra.

Comparison Bars are used to solve problems that involve one amount that is more than or less than another amount. Drawing Comparison Bars can help a student organize the information in the problem in order to find the unknown smaller amount, the unknown larger amount, or the difference.

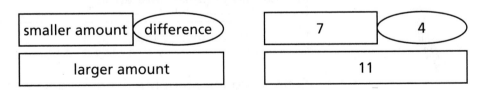

smaller amount	difference
larger amount	

7	4
11	

Please call or write if you have any questions or comments.

Sincerely,
Your child's teacher

COMMON CORE This unit includes the Common Core Standards for Mathematical Content for Operations and Algebraic Thinking, CC.3.OA.3, CC.3.OA.4, CC.3.OA.8; Numbers and Operations in Base Ten, CC.3.NBT.1, CC.3.NBT.2, CC.3.NBT.3 and for all Mathematical Practices.

Estimada familia:

En esta unidad, su niño resolverá sumas, restas, multiplicaciones y divisiones con sumandos o factores desconocidos.

Muestra a tu familia la Carta a la familia de la página 160 del Cuaderno de actividades y trabajo.

- Si uno de los sumandos se desconoce, puede hallarse restando el sumando conocido del total, o contando hacia adelante desde el sumando conocido hasta llegar al total.
- Si el total se desconoce, puede hallarse sumando los sumandos.
- Si uno de los factores se desconoce, puede hallarse dividiendo el producto entre el otro factor.
- Si el producto se desconoce, puede hallarse multiplicando los factores.

Para mostrar un total y dos sumandos se usan las **Montañas matemáticas**. Los estudiantes puede usarlas para escribir una ecuación, y al resolverla, hallar el elemento desconocido.

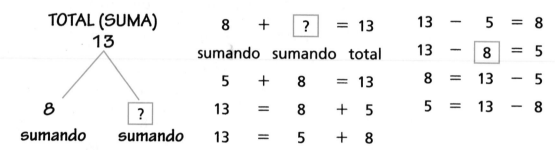

Se hace énfasis en las ecuaciones que tienen números solos en el lado izquierdo, para facilitar la comprensión del álgebra.

Para resolver problemas con una cantidad que es más o menos que otra, se usan **Barras de comparación**. Estas barras sirven para organizar la información del problema, y hallar así, la cantidad desconocida más pequeña, la más grande o la diferencia.

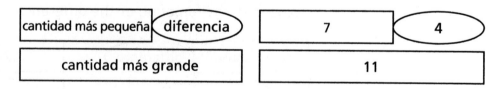

Si tiene alguna pregunta o algún comentario, por favor comuníquese conmigo.

Atentamente,
El maestro de su niño

COMMON CORE

Esta unidad incluye los Common Core Standards for Mathematical Content for Operations and Algebraic Thinking, CC.3.OA.3, CC.3.OA.4, CC.3.OA.8; Numbers and Operations in Base Ten, CC.3.NBT.1, CC.3.NBT.2, CC.3.NBT.3 and for all Mathematical Practices.

Addition and Subtraction Situations

Show your work on your paper or in your journal.

VOCABULARY
total
addend
sum

▶ Math Mountains and Equations

Complete.

1. Look at the Math Mountain and the 8 equations. What relationships do you see? In each equation, label each number as an **addend** (*A*) or the **total** (*T*).

sum
total
110

70   40
addend   addend

$$110 = 70 + 40 \qquad 70 + 40 = 110$$

$$110 = 40 + 70 \qquad 40 + 70 = 110$$

$$40 = 110 - 70 \qquad 110 - 70 = 40$$

$$70 = 110 - 40 \qquad 110 - 40 = 70$$

2. Write the 8 equations for this Math Mountain. Label each number as the total (*T*) or an addend (*A*).

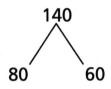

140

80   60

▶ **Solve and Discuss**

Show your work
on your paper or
in your journal.

Solve each problem. Label your answers.

3. **Add To** Chris's group picked 80 apples.
   His mother's group picked 60 more.
   How many apples do they have now?

4. **Take From** Chris's group had 140 apples.
   They ate 80 of them. How many apples
   do they have now?

5. **Put Together/Take Apart** Alison's class
   brought 70 juice boxes to the picnic.
   Taylor's class brought 50 juice boxes.
   How many juice boxes did they bring
   altogether?

6. **Put Together/Take Apart** There are 120 juice
   boxes at the picnic. Alison puts 70 on tables
   and leaves the rest in the cooler. How many
   juice boxes are in the cooler?

Addition and Subtraction Situations

▶ Represent Word Problems with Math Tools

The equations and Math Mountains below
show the word problems on page 260.

Add To

80   +   60   =   ■

Chris's   Mom's   total
group   group

■
╱ ╲
80   60

Take From

140   −   80   =   ■

total   ate   now
(sum)

140
╱ ╲
80   ■

Put Together/Take Apart

70   +   50   =   ■

Alison's   Taylor's   total
class   class

■
╱ ╲
70   50

Put Together/Take Apart

120   −   70   =   ■

total   tables   cooler

70   +   ■   =   120

tables   cooler   total

120
╱ ╲
70   ■

7. Write the unknown numbers in the boxes.

8. How are these math tools the same?
   How are they different?

9. **Math Journal** Write a word problem for this
   equation: 110 − 40 = ■. Then solve it.

VOCABULARY
expression
equation

▶ (PATH to FLUENCY) **Discuss the = and ≠ Signs**

An **expression** is a combination of numbers, variables, and/or operation signs. Expressions do not have an equal sign.

An **equation** is made up of two equal quantities or expressions. An equal sign (=) is used to show that the two sides are equal.

$$8 = 5 + 3 \qquad 4 + 2 = 6 \qquad 7 = 7 \qquad 3 + 2 = 2 + 3 \qquad 6 - 2 = 1 + 1 + 2$$

The "is not equal to" sign (≠) shows that two quantities are not equal.

$$7 \neq 5 + 3 \qquad 4 + 2 \neq 8 \qquad 7 \neq 6 \qquad 6 - 2 \neq 2 + 3 \qquad 5 + 2 \neq 1 + 1 + 3$$

10. Use the = sign to write four equations. Vary how many numbers you have on each side of the sign.

11. Use the ≠ sign to write four "is not equal to" statements. Vary how many numbers you have on each side of the sign.

Write a number to make the number sentence true.

12. $160 = \blacksquare + 90$

13. $30 + \blacksquare \neq 120$

14. $70 + 20 = 20 + \blacksquare$

15. $150 - \blacksquare = 70$

16. $\blacksquare \neq 140 - 70$

17. $60 - 20 \neq 10 + 10 + \blacksquare$

Write = or ≠ to make a true number sentence.

18. $80 + 20 + 40 \,\blacksquare\, 90 + 50$

19. $80 \,\blacksquare\, 60 - 20$

20. $70 \,\blacksquare\, 40 + 30$

Show your work on your paper or in your journal.

▶ Solve Unknown Addend Word Problems

Draw a Math Mountain and write and label an equation with a variable. Then solve each problem.

1. **Put Together/Take Apart:**
   Unknown Addend Stacy invited 90 girls and some boys to her party. 160 children were invited in all. How many boys were invited?

2. **Put Together/Take Apart:**
   Unknown Addend There were 150 people at the park. 70 were playing soccer. The others were playing softball. How many people were playing softball?

3. **Add To: Unknown Addend** Jan planted 80 tulips last week. Today she planted some lilies. Now she has 170 flowers. How many lilies did she plant?

4. **Take From: Unknown Addend** Tim's team had 140 tennis balls. Then his brother's team borrowed some. Now Tim's team has 60 tennis balls. How many did his brother's team borrow?

► Represent Unknown Addends with Math Tools

The equations and Math Mountains below show
the word problems on page 263.

Put Together/Take Apart:
Unknown Addend

$$90 \quad + \quad b \quad = \quad 160$$
girls   boys   children

children
160

90   ▪
girls   boys

Put Together/Take Apart:
Unknown Addend

$$150 \quad - \quad s \quad = \quad 70$$
park   softball   soccer

park
150

▪   70
softball   soccer

Add To: Unknown Addend

$$80 \quad + \quad l \quad = \quad 170$$
tulips   lilies   flowers

flowers
170

80   ▪
tulips   lilies

Take From: Unknown Addend

$$140 \quad - \quad n \quad = \quad 60$$
balls   some   now

balls
140

▪   60
some   now

5. Write the unknown numbers in the boxes and above the variables.

6. How are these math tools alike? How are they different?

▶ Solve Unknown Factor Word Problems

Write an equation for each word problem.
Use a variable to represent the unknown
factor. Then solve the problem.

7. A toymaker has 36 boxes of toy trains to
   ship to 4 toy shops. Each shop will get the
   same number of boxes. How many boxes
   of toy trains will each shop get?

8. There are 56 cars in a parking lot. There are
   8 rows and the same number of cars is in
   each row. How many cars are in each row?

9. An apartment building has 42 apartments.
   There are 6 apartments on each floor.
   How many floors are in the apartment building?

10. There are 48 students in the marching band.
    The students stand in equal rows of 8.
    How many rows of students are there?

▶ Solve Unknown Factor Word Problems (continued)

Write an equation for each word problem. Use a variable to represent the unknown factor. Then solve the problem.

11. Daniel is setting up seats for the third grade play. There are 6 seats in each row. There are 54 seats in all. How many rows of seats are there?

12. Mrs. Martinez is sewing buttons on 4 costumes. Each costume has the same number of buttons. There are 32 buttons in all. How many buttons are on each costume?

13. The library received 63 new books. The librarian will put 7 books on each shelf. How many shelves are there?

14. There are 72 juice boxes for the class picnic. The juice boxes are in packs of 8. How many packs of juice boxes are there?

Show your work
on your paper or
in your journal.

▶ Solve Unknown Start Problems

Solve each problem. Label your answers.

1. **Add To: Unknown Start** Greta puts some beads on a string. Then she puts on 70 more beads. Now there are 130 beads on the string. How many beads did she put on the string to start?

2. **Take From: Unknown Start** Greta puts some beads on a string. Seventy of the beads fell off the string. Sixty beads are still on the string. How many beads were there at first?

3. **Add To: Unknown Start** Patrick was carrying some booklets. His teacher asked him to carry 30 more booklets. Now he has 110 booklets. How many booklets did he start with?

4. **Take From: Unknown Start** Patricia was carrying some pencils. Her friend took 30 of them. Patricia has 80 pencils left. How many pencils was she carrying at first?

▶ Represent Unknown Start Problems with Math Tools

The equations and Math Mountains below show the word problems on page 267.

Add To: Unknown Start

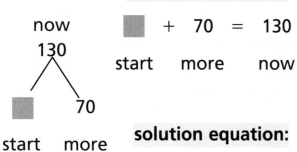

situation equation:

▢ + 70 = 130

start   more   now

solution equation:

70 + ▢ = 130

130 − 70 = ▢

Take From: Unknown Start

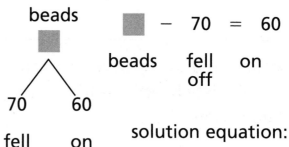

situation equation:

▢ − 70 = 60

beads   fell   on
         off

solution equation:

60 + 70 = ▢

Add To: Unknown Start

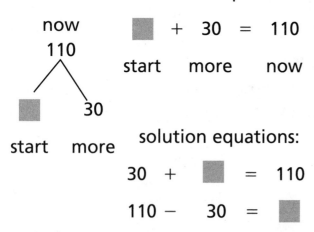

situation equation:

▢ + 30 = 110

start   more   now

solution equations:

30 + ▢ = 110

110 − 30 = ▢

Take From: Unknown Start

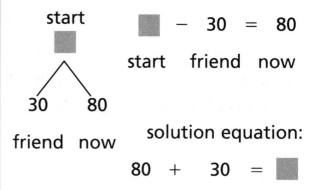

situation equation:

▢ − 30 = 80

start   friend   now

solution equation:

80 + 30 = ▢

5. Write the unknown numbers in the boxes.

6. How are these math tools alike? How are they different?

▶ Write Situation and Solution Equations

**Write a situation equation and a solution equation.
Then solve the problem.**

7. Eight vans with the same number of students
in each van took 40 students to the science center
for a field trip. How many students were in each van?

   Situation Equation:

   Solution Equation:

8. Fiona made some barrettes. She put 9 beads
on each barrette. If she used 63 beads, how many
barrettes did she make?

   Situation Equation:

   Solution Equation:

9. The pet store has 81 birds. There are 9 birds in
each cage. How many cages are there?

   Situation Equation:

   Solution Equation:

10. Enrique has 56 miniature cars. He put the
same number of cars on 7 shelves in his
room. How many cars are on each shelf?

    Situation Equation:

    Solution Equation:

▶ Write Situation and Solution Equations (continued)

**Write a situation equation and a solution equation.
Then solve the problem.**

11. A group of 48 students from 8 schools are competing in the science fair. Each school sends the same number of students. How many students are competing from each school?

    Situation Equation:

    Solution Equation:

12. An array on one wall in an art gallery has 27 photographs. Each row has 9 photographs. How many rows are there?

    Situation Equation:

    Solution Equation:

13. Jody bought 4 bags of lemons to make lemonade. The same number of lemons was in each bag. There were a total of 36 lemons. How many lemons were in each bag?

    Situation Equation:

    Solution Equation:

14. A hardware store sold a number of furnace filters. There were 6 filters in each box. If they sold 54 furnace filters, how many boxes of filters did the hardware store sell?

    Situation Equation:

    Solution Equation:

► Compare Numbers

Compare the numbers. Write >, < or = in each ⬤.

1. 34 ⬤ 86

2. 97 ⬤ 67

3. 653 ⬤ 663

4. 875 ⬤ 587

5. 752 ⬤ 572

6. 864 ⬤ 846

7. 1,932 ⬤ 2,951

8. 2,633 ⬤ 2,487

9. 3,478 ⬤ 3,478

10. 4,786 ⬤ 4,876

► Order Numbers

Write the numbers in order from greatest to least.

11. 69, 20, 81

12. 381, 124, 197

Write the numbers in order from least to greatest.

13. 2,245, 1,642, 787

14. 1,987, 1,898, 1,789

VOCABULARY
comparison bars

▶ **Discuss Comparison Problems**

Solve each problem. Label your answers.

David has 5 marbles. Ana has 8 marbles.

15. How many more marbles
    does Ana have than David?

16. How many fewer marbles
    does David have than Ana?

Here are two ways to represent the comparison situation.

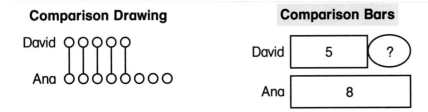

Claire has 8 marbles. Sasha has 15 marbles.

17. How many more marbles does
    Sasha have than Claire?

18. How many fewer marbles does
    Claire have than Sasha?

Rocky has 7 fishing lures. Megan has 12
fishing lures.

19. How many fewer fishing
    lures does Rocky have
    than Megan?

Show your work on your paper or in your journal.

▶ Comparison Problems With an Unknown Larger or Smaller Amount

Solve each problem. Label your answers.

20. **Unknown Larger Amount** Maribel has 18 stickers. Arnon has 13 more stickers than Maribel. How many stickers does Arnon have?

21. **Unknown Smaller Amount** Arnon has 31 stickers. Maribel has 13 fewer stickers than Arnon. How many stickers does Maribel have?

22. **Unknown Larger Amount** Ivan has 19 goldfish. Milo has 15 more goldfish than Ivan. How many goldfish does Milo have?

23. **Unknown Smaller Amount** Milo has 34 goldfish. Ivan has 15 fewer goldfish than Milo. How many goldfish does Ivan have?

Show your work on your paper or in your journal.

▶ Use Comparison Bars to Represent an Unknown Amount

Solve each problem. Label your answers.

24. **Unknown Smaller Amount** T.J. has 18 fewer miniature cars than Corey. Corey has 32 miniature cars. How many miniature cars does T.J. have?

25. **Unknown Larger Amount** Corey has 18 more miniature cars than T.J. T.J. has 14 miniature cars. How many miniature cars does Corey have?

26. **Unknown Smaller Amount** Grace has 19 fewer stuffed animals than Sophia. Sophia has 31 stuffed animals. How many stuffed animals does Grace have?

27. **Unknown Larger Amount** Sophia has 19 more stuffed animals than Grace. Grace has 12 stuffed animals. How many stuffed animals does Sophia have?

► What's the Error?

Dear Math Students,

As part of my math homework, I solved this problem:

Carlos has 19 fish. He has 14 fewer fish than Daniel. How many fish does Daniel have?

Here is what I did: 19 − 14 = 5   Daniel has 5 fish.

Carlos | 19 |
Daniel | ? | 14 |

Is my answer right? If not, please correct my work, and tell me what I did wrong.

Your friend,
Puzzled Penguin

1. Write an answer to Puzzled Penguin.

► Solve Comparison Problems with Misleading Language

Solve each problem on a separate piece of paper.

2. **Unknown Smaller Amount** Daniel has 23 fish. He has 15 more fish than Carlos. How many fish does Carlos have?

3. **Unknown Larger Amount** Gina ran 12 laps. She ran 8 fewer laps than Bettina. How many laps did Bettina run?

4. **Unknown Smaller Amount** Bettina ran 20 laps. She ran 8 more laps than Gina. How many laps did Gina run?

5. **Unknown Larger Amount** Sara read 18 books this month. She read 13 fewer books than Lupe. How many books did Lupe read this month?

Show your work
on your paper or
in your journal.

► Solve Comparison Problems Without the Words *More* or *Fewer*

Solve each problem. Label your answers.

6. The coach brought 18 hockey sticks to practice. There were 23 players at practice. How many players didn't get sticks?

7. At a meeting, 15 people had to stand because there were not enough chairs. There were 12 chairs. How many people came to the meeting?

8. Jess had 16 apples. After he gave one to each of his cousins, he had 13 apples left. How many cousins does Jess have?

9. At the park, 4 of the children could not swing because there were not enough swings. There were 20 children at the park. How many swings were on the swing set?

10. Maile took one step on each tile along the garden path. After she took 14 steps, there were 13 more tiles left to go. How many tiles were there along the path?

Comparison Problems with Misleading Language

► **Solve Problems with Extra Information**

Write any extra information on your paper or in your journal.

Read each problem. Cross out any extra information. Then solve.

1. Emma solved 9 math problems and answered 7 reading questions. Her sister solved 8 math problems. How many math problems did they solve in all?

2. Mark had 6 shirts and 5 pairs of pants. Today his aunt gave him 4 more shirts and another pair of pants. How many shirts does he have now?

3. A parking lot had 179 cars and 95 trucks. Then 85 cars left the lot. How many cars are in the parking lot now?

4. Laura had some roses in a vase. From her garden, she picked 7 more roses and 6 daisies. Now she has 12 roses in all. How many roses did she have at first?

5. Nikko had 245 pennies and 123 nickels. His brother gave him 89 more pennies and 25 more nickels. How many pennies does Nikko have now?

Write the hidden information on your paper or in your journal.

▶ Solve Problems with Hidden Information

Read each problem. Circle the hidden information. Then solve.

6. Samuel had 16 horseshoes in the shed yesterday. Today he put a new set of horseshoes on his horse Betsy. How many horseshoes are left in the shed?

7. Maya is going on a vacation with her family for a week and 3 days. How many days will she be on vacation?

8. Julie bought a dozen eggs at the market. She gave 3 of them to Serge. How many eggs does Julie have left?

9. Lisa had 3 quarters and 2 dimes. Then she found 3 nickels and 12 pennies. What is the value of the coins in cents she has now?

10. Marissa is moving away. She is going to move back in a year and 21 days. How many days will she be gone?

► Recognize Word Problems with Not Enough Information

Tell what information is needed to solve each problem.

11. Sara bought 8 bananas at the fruit market. She put them in a bowl with some oranges. How many pieces of fruit are in the bowl?

12. Rebecca did 112 dives in competition last summer. This summer, she did many more dives in competition. How many competition dives did she do in the two summers?

13. Meg bought 3 mystery books and put them on the shelf with her other mystery books. How many mystery books are now on the shelf?

14. Our school has 5 soccer balls, 6 basketballs, and 4 footballs. Today, some of the footballs were lost. How many balls does the school have now?

▶ Solve Word Problems with Not Enough Information

If more information is needed, rewrite the problem to include the necessary information. Then solve it.

15. Leah began fishing at 2:00 in the afternoon. She stopped at dinnertime. How many hours did Leah fish?

16. The train traveled 376 miles on Tuesday. It traveled even more miles on Wednesday. How many miles did the train travel on Tuesday and Wednesday?

17. The Kitchen Store sold 532 pans and 294 pots. Then some pans were returned. How many pans were not returned?

18. Julio and Scott played 6 card games and 4 computer games today. How many hours did they play games?

Word Problems with Extra, Hidden, or Not Enough Information

▶ Write First Step Questions

Write the first step question and answer.
Then solve the problem.

1. The orchard has 8 rows of apple trees. There are
   7 rows with 6 apple trees and one row with 4 apple
   trees. How many apple trees are in the orchard?

2. Ms. Hayes bought 4 packs of pencils with 10 pencils in
   each pack. She divided the pencils evenly among her
   5 children. How many pencils did each child get?

3. Kylen made 30 necklaces and gave 6 away. She put
   the rest in 4 boxes with an equal number in each
   box. How many necklaces were in each box?

4. Libby had 42 vacation pictures and 12 birthday pictures.
   She put an equal number of pictures on 9 pages in her
   scrapbook. How many pictures did Libby put on each page?

5. Mr. Cerda bought 9 boxes of tiles. Each box had 8 tiles.
   He used all but 5 of the tiles. How many tiles did
   Mr. Cerda use?

► Write First Step Questions (continued)

Write the first step question and answer.
Then solve the problem.

6. A bus has 10 seats that can each hold 2 passengers and another seat that can hold 3 passengers. How many passengers can be seated on the bus?

7. Dana made 6 fruit baskets. She put 4 apples, 2 pears, and 3 oranges in each basket. How many pieces of fruit did Dana use in all?

8. Cecilia ordered 5 pizzas for a group of friends. Each pizza had 8 slices. All but 3 slices were eaten. How many slices were eaten?

9. Randall has 122 coins in his collection. Fifty coins are quarters and the rest are nickels. If he fills 9 pages in a coin folder with the same number of nickels, how many nickels are on each page?

10. Lindsey made 6 bracelets. She used a total of 60 beads. Each bracelet has 6 beads that are silver and the rest are blue. How many beads on each bracelet are blue?

► What's the Error?

Dear Math Students, My teacher gave me this problem:

Luther had 11 sheets of colored paper. 6 were orange, and the rest were blue. Today he used 2 sheets of blue paper. How many sheets of blue paper does Luther have now?

Here is what I did: 11 – 6 = 5
Luther now has 5 blue sheets.

Is my answer correct? If not, please correct my work and tell me what I did wrong.

Your friend,
Puzzled Penguin

1. Write an answer to Puzzled Penguin.

► Solve Two Step Word Problems

Solve each problem. Label your answers.

2. The Hillside bus had 14 passengers. When it stopped, 5 people got off and 8 people got on. How many people are riding the Hillside bus now?

3. There are 15 fish in a tank. 12 are goldfish, and the others are angelfish. How many more goldfish are there than angelfish?

▶ Solve and Discuss

Solve each problem. Label your answers.

4. Sun Mi picked 14 apricots. Celia picked 5 fewer apricots than Sun Mi. How many apricots did Sun Mi and Celia pick altogether?

5. Annie took 8 photographs at home and 7 photographs at school. Her sister Amanda took 6 fewer photographs than Annie. How many photographs did Amanda take?

6. There are 5 mice, 3 gerbils, and some hamsters in a cage. Altogether there are 15 animals in the cage. How many hamsters are there?

7. A new library opened on Saturday. The library lent out 234 books on Saturday. On Sunday, they lent out 138 books. That day, 78 books were returned. How many books were not returned?

8. Katie had 8 dimes and some nickels in her duck bank. She had 4 more nickels than dimes. She took out 5 nickels to buy a newspaper. How many nickels are in her duck bank now?

9. Tony had 14 colored pencils. 9 of them needed sharpening, and the rest were sharp. Yesterday, his uncle gave him some new colored pencils. Now Tony has 12 sharp colored pencils. How many colored pencils did his uncle give him?

▶ Is the Answer Reasonable?

Use rounding or mental math to decide if the answer is reasonable. Write *yes* or *no*. Then write an equation and solve the problem to see if you were correct.

10. Chelsea's class collected cans of food for their local food pantry. They collected 27 cans on Monday and 78 cans on Tuesday. Then on Wednesday they collected 53 cans. How many cans did the class collect on those three days?
    Answer: 158 cans

11. Barry strings beads. He had 54 beads on a string and he took off 29 beads. Then he took off 5 more. How many beads are on the string now?
    Answer: 35 beads

12. Dena counted the books on three shelves of the classroom library. She counted 33 books on the top shelf, 52 books on the middle shelf, and 48 books on the bottom shelf. How many books are on the three shelves?
    Answer: 163 books

13. Ms. Lance bought 6 packages of paper cups. Each package has 20 cups. She used 78 cups for a party. How many cups does Ms. Lance have left?
    Answer: 58 cups

▶ Reasonable Answers

Use rounding or mental math to decide if the answer is reasonable. Write *yes* or *no*. Then write an equation and solve the problem to see if you were correct.

14. There were 83 students in a spelling contest. In the first round 9 students were eliminated. Then 29 students were eliminated during the second round. How many students were left for the third round?
    Answer: 24 students

15. During one week Tina rode her bicycle 42 miles and Jim rode 9 fewer miles than Tina. How many miles did they ride altogether that week?
    Answer: 75 miles

16. Rusty volunteers at her local animal shelter. It costs $10 a day to care for a cat or dog in the shelter. The total cost to care for the animals one day was $90. There were 5 dogs at the shelter and the rest were cats. How many cats were at the shelter that day?
    Answer: 9 cats

17. Jake is saving money for a new bike that costs $187. He saved $55 one month and $44 the next month. How much more money does Jake need to buy the bike?
    Answer: $88

► Equations and Two Step Word Problems

Write an equation and solve the problem.

1. Mrs. Delgado is baking pies and cakes for a school fundraiser. She bought 26 apples, 29 peaches, and a number of bananas at the Farmers' Market. She bought 66 pieces of fruit. How many bananas did she buy?

2. Abby bought 8 packages of stickers with the same number of stickers in each package. She gave 15 stickers to her sister. Now Abby has 49 stickers. How many stickers were in each package?

3. Taylor is reading a 340-page book. He read 174 pages of the book on Saturday and 120 pages on Sunday. How many pages does he have left to read?

4. Lauren had a piece of ribbon that was 36 inches long. She cut a number of 3-inch pieces. She has 15 inches of ribbon left. How many 3-inch pieces did she cut?

5. There are 47 students in the marching band. There are 5 students in the first row, and the rest are in equal rows of 6. How many students are in each of the 6 rows?

▶ Solve Two Step Word Problems

Write an equation and solve the problem.

6. Sara's mother baked 48 cookies. Sara gave a dozen cookies to her neighbor and divided the remaining cookies on plates of 9 cookies each. How many plates did she use?

7. Marissa is making floral bouquets. She bought 56 carnations, 73 chrysanthemums, and some roses. She bought 153 flowers in all. How many roses did she buy?

8. Thomas has 103 photos on his digital camera. He deletes 33 because they are out of focus. He wants to print the remaining photos and put an equal number on each page of an album that has 10 pages. How many photos will be on each page?

9. Leo bought 6 sets of books. Each set had the same number of books. He donated 11 books to the school library. Now he has 37 books left. How many books were in each set of books Leo bought?

10. Amber has 5 packages of chalk. Each package has 9 pieces of chalk. She gave a number of pieces of chalk to her brother. Amber has 37 pieces of chalk left. How many pieces did Amber give her brother?

▶ Write Two Step Equations

Write an equation and solve the problem.

1. Carrie sold 7 toys for 50¢ each and 1 toy for 75¢. How much money, in cents, did Carrie make?

2. Darin earns $8 each week doing chores. He is saving his money to buy a game that costs $49 and a cap that costs $15. How many weeks will Darin need to save his money?

3. A dog trainer is working with 7 dogs. He rewards each dog with the same number of treats. He started with 35 treats and he has 7 left. How many treats did he give each dog?

4. Sheila has two dogs. One dog weighs 46 pounds and her other dog weighs 14 pounds more. How many pounds do the two dogs weigh altogether?

5. Eli has 36 stamps and his brother has 24 stamps. They put their stamps in the same book. They put the same number of stamps on each page. They used 10 pages. How many stamps are on each page?

▶ Write Two Step Equations (continued)

Write an equation and solve the problem.

6. There were 9 rows of chairs set up in the school gym. Each row had 20 chairs. After the students were seated, there were 12 empty chairs. How many chairs were filled?

7. Eric had 143 baseball cards. His uncle gave him a number more. Then Eric gave 26 cards to a friend. He has 184 cards now. How many cards did Eric's uncle give him?

8. Brandi had 8 equal rows of stickers. She bought 5 more and now she has 53 stickers. How many were in each row before she bought more?

9. Randall cut a board into two pieces. One piece has a length of 84 inches. The other piece is 24 inches shorter. How long was the board Randall cut?

10. A science poster shows 9 insects with 6 legs each and a spider with 8 legs. How many legs is that altogether?

► **Math and News**

**Little League Baseball Championships:
Wheaton Wolves Score Win**

Wheaton Wolves win Little
League World Series Championship.
The chart shows some statistics from
the six games the team played.

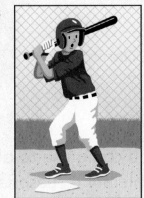

Wheaton Wolves Statistics	
Times at Bat	155
Hits	47
Base on Balls	25
Runs Scored	36
Strike Outs	36

**Use the information in the table to write an equation
and solve the problem.**

1. How many times at bat did players not strike
   out or get a base on balls?

2. How many hits and base on balls did not result
   in a run?

3. The Wheaton Wolves had 13 triple or double-base
   hits, 3 homeruns, and the rest were single-base hits.
   How many single-base hits did the team get?

▶ Sports News

Danielle plays on a third grade basketball team in a league. Her team made the news when they scored 47 points, 41 points, and 53 points in a three-game tournament.

Write a two step equation and solve the problem.

4. How many points did Danielle's team score altogether?

5. Describe a method you could use to decide if your answer to Problem 4 is reasonable.

6. Danielle's scorecard shows her statistics for the three games. Use the information in the table to write equations to find the unknown numbers. Then complete the table.

	Number of 1-pt Free Throws	**Number of 2-pt Field Goals**	**Total Points**
Game 1	5	7	
Game 2		6	18
Game 3	3		21

Focus on Mathematical Practices

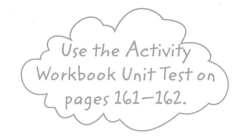

Use the Activity
Workbook Unit Test on
pages 161–162.

► Vocabulary

Choose the best word from the box.

1. An ____?____ is a mathematical sentence with an equal sign. (Lesson 5-1)

2. The ____?____ is the answer when adding two or more addends. (Lesson 5-1)

3. One of the numbers to be added is called a (an) ____?____. (Lesson 5-1)

► Concepts and Skills

Complete.

4. Elsa read 13 books this month.
   She read 6 fewer books than Cliff read.
   How many books did Cliff read?
   Draw comparison bars to represent
   the problem. (Lessons 5-4, 5-5)

5. Mr. Jackson set up some chairs in rows. He put the same number in each of 7 rows and put 7 chairs in the last row. He set up 70 chairs. How many did he put in each of the 7 rows? Explain how to write an equation and solve the problem. (Lessons 5-8, 5-9, 5-10, 5-11)

Complete.

6. Julie and Sam grew tomatoes. Julie grew
160 plants. How many more tomatoes did Julie
grow than Sam? What information do you need to
solve the problem? Write the necessary information
and solve the problem. (Lesson 5-6)

▶ Problem Solving

Write an equation and solve the problem.
(Lessons 5-6, 5-8, 5-9, 5-10, 5-11)

7. Becky has 20 fish and 2 hamsters. There are 8 angelfish and the rest are goldfish. She gets a number more goldfish. She now has 19 goldfish. How many goldfish did she get?

8. Raj is going on vacation for 2 weeks and 5 days. How many days will he be on vacation?

9. Paco made 33 belts and gave 5 away. He put the rest on 7 hangers with an equal number on each hanger. How many belts are on each hanger?

10. **Extended Response** Jason has 452 toy dinosaurs in his collection. His sister gave him 38 more toy dinosaurs. He sold a number of them. He now has 418 toy dinosaurs. How many did he sell? Explain how you can decide if your answer is reasonable.

Dear Family,

Your student will be learning about geometry and measurement during this school year. This first part of Unit 6 is about the geometric figures called quadrilaterals. These get their name because they have four (*quad-*) sides (*-lateral*).

Here are some examples of quadrilaterals students will be learning about in this unit.

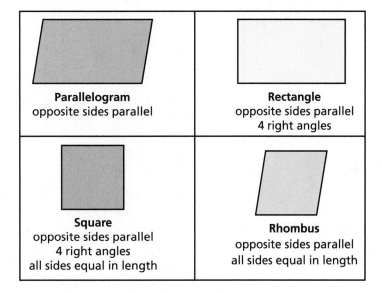

Parallelogram
opposite sides parallel

Rectangle
opposite sides parallel
4 right angles

Square
opposite sides parallel
4 right angles
all sides equal in length

Rhombus
opposite sides parallel
all sides equal in length

> Share with your family the Family Letter on Activity Workbook page 163.

Students will be able to recognize and describe different quadrilaterals by their sides and angles. Some sides may be of equal length. Some sides may be parallel; they do not meet no matter how far they are extended. Some sides may be perpendicular; where they meet is like the corner of a square.

If you have any questions, please call or write to me.

Thank you.

Sincerely,
Your child's teacher

COMMON CORE   This unit includes the Common Core Standards for Mathematical Content for Geometry, 3.G.1 and 3.G.2, and all Mathematical Practices.

Estimada familia:

Durante este año escolar, su niño aprenderá acerca de geometría y medición. La primera parte de la Unidad 6 trata sobre las figuras geométricas llamadas cuadriláteros. Se llaman así porque tienen cuatro (*quadri-*) lados (*-lateris*).

Aquí se muestran algunos ejemplos de cuadriláteros que los estudiantes estudiarán en esta unidad.

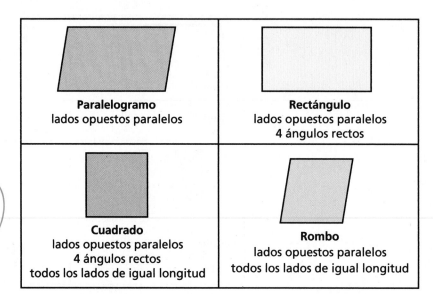

Paralelogramo
lados opuestos paralelos

Rectángulo
lados opuestos paralelos
4 ángulos rectos

Cuadrado
lados opuestos paralelos
4 ángulos rectos
todos los lados de igual longitud

Rombo
lados opuestos paralelos
todos los lados de igual longitud

Muestra a tu familia la Carta a la familia de la página 164 del Cuaderno de actividades y trabajo.

Los estudiantes podrán reconocer y describir diferentes cuadriláteros según sus lados y ángulos. Algunos lados pueden tener la misma longitud. Algunos lados pueden ser paralelos; nunca se juntan, no importa cuánto se extiendan. Algunos lados pueden ser perpendiculares; donde se juntan es como el vértice de un cuadrado.

Si tiene alguna pregunta o algún comentario, por favor comuníquese conmigo.

Gracias.

Atentamente,
El maestro de su niño

COMMON CORE Esta unidad incluye los Common Core Standards for Mathematical Content for Geometry, 3.G.1 and 3.G.2, and all Mathematical Practices.

VOCABULARY
ray
angle
right angle

► Types of Angles

A **ray** is part of a line that has one endpoint and
continues forever in one direction. To draw
a ray, make an arrow to show that it goes on forever.

Two line segments or two rays that meet at
an endpoint form an **angle**.

   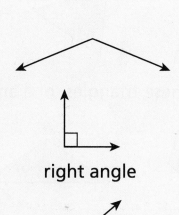

An angle that forms a square corner is
called a **right angle**.

right angle

Some angles are smaller than a right angle.

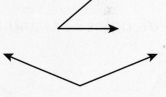

Some angles are larger than a right angle.

These angles are named with a letter in the corner.

 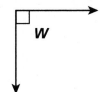 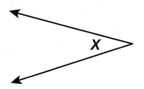 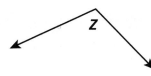

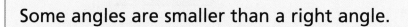

1. Which of the angles are right angles?

2. Which of the angles are smaller than a right angle?

3. Which of the angles are larger than a right angle?

VOCABULARY
triangle

► Describe Triangles by Types of Angles

Triangles can be described by the types of angles they have.

In these triangles, one angle is a right angle.

 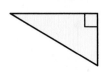 

In these triangles, three angles are smaller than a right angle.

In these triangles, one angle is larger than a right angle.

 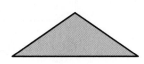 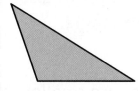

Use triangles *K*, *L*, and *M* for Exercises 4–6.

 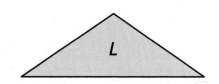 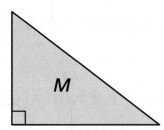

4. Which triangle has one right angle?

5. Which triangle has three angles smaller than a right angle?

6. Which triangle has one angle larger than a right angle?

► Describe Triangles by the Number of Sides of Equal Length

You can also describe triangles by the number of sides that are of equal length.

In these triangles, three sides are equal in length.

In these triangles, two sides are equal in length.

 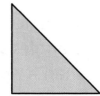 

In these triangles, no sides are equal in length.

  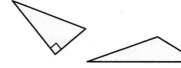

Use triangles *B*, *C*, and *D* for Exercises 7–9.

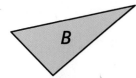

7. Which triangle has 3 sides of equal length?

8. Which triangle has 2 sides of equal length?

9. Which triangle has 0 sides of equal length?

► ## Describe Triangles by Types of Angles and Number of Sides of Equal Length

Use triangles *M*, *N*, and *O* for 10–12. Write *M*, *N*, or *O*. Then complete the sentences.

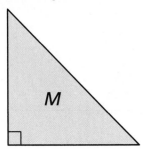 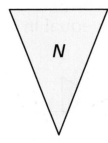 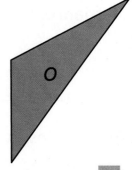

10. Triangle _____ has 1 angle larger than a right angle and has _____ sides of equal length.

11. Triangle _____ has 1 right angle and has _____ sides of equal length.

12. Triangle _____ has 3 angles smaller than a right angle and has _____ sides of equal length.

Use triangles *P*, *Q*, and *R* for 13–15. Write *P*, *Q*, or *R*. Then complete the sentences.

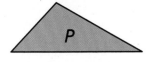 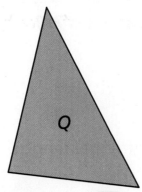 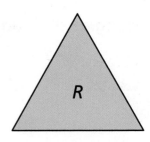

13. Triangle _____ has 3 angles smaller than a right angle and has _____ sides of equal length.

14. Triangle _____ has 3 angles smaller than a right angle and has _____ sides of equal length.

15. Triangle _____ has 1 angle larger than a right angle and has _____ sides of equal length.

VOCABULARY
polygon
concave
convex

► Polygons

A **polygon** is a flat, closed figure made up of line segments that do not cross each other.

Circle the figures that are polygons.

16.

17.

18.

19.

20.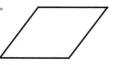

21.

22.

23.

A figure can be **concave** or **convex**. In concave polygons, there exists a line segment with endpoints inside the polygon and a point on the line segment that is outside the polygon. A convex figure has no such line segment.

concave   convex

Which figures are convex and which are concave?

24.

25.

26.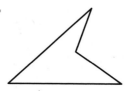

27.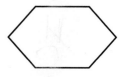

VOCABULARY

pentagon   hexagon
octagon   decagon

► Name Polygons

Polygons are named according to how many sides they have.

3 sides – **tri**angle   4 sides – **quad**rilateral   5 sides – **penta**gon

6 sides – **hexa**gon   8 sides – **octa**gon   10 sides – **deca**gon

Name each figure.

28.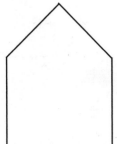

29.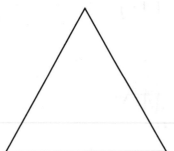

30.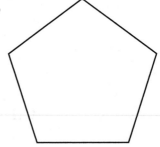

31.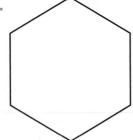

32.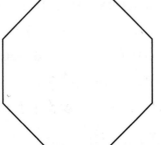

33.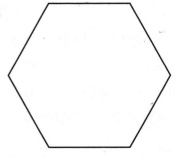

34.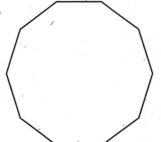

35.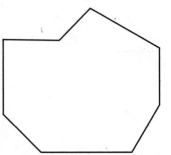

36.

Triangles

▶ Describe Parallelograms

All of these figures are **parallelograms**.

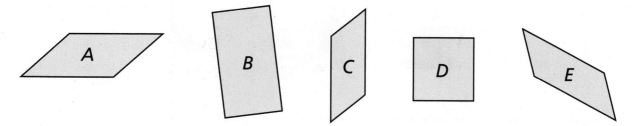

These figures are not parallelograms.

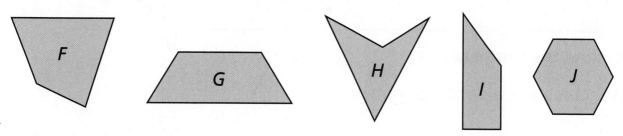

Complete the sentence.

1. A parallelogram is a quadrilateral with

▶ Measure Sides of Parallelograms

For each parallelogram, measure the sides to the nearest cm and label them with their lengths.

2.   3.   4.

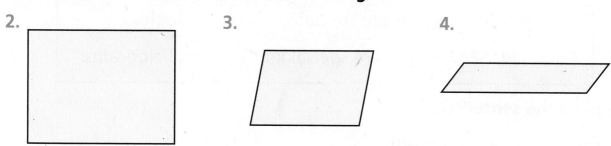

5. Look at the lengths of the sides. What patterns do you notice?

VOCABULARY
rectangle
square
rhombus

▶ Describe Rectangles

All of these figures are **rectangles**.

Adel said, "Rectangles are special kinds of parallelograms."

Complete the sentence.

6. A rectangle is a parallelogram with

▶ Explore Squares and Rhombuses

These figures are **squares**.   These figures are **rhombuses**.

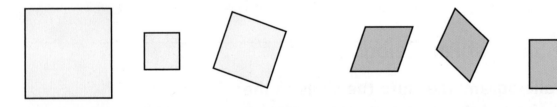

Takeshi said, "Squares are special kinds of rectangles."

Cora said, "Rhombuses are special kinds of parallelograms."

Complete the sentence.

7. A square is a rectangle with

8. A rhombus is a parallelogram with

▶ Describe Quadrilaterals

Use as many words below as possible to describe
each figure.

| quadrilateral | parallelogram | rectangle | square |

9.

10.

11.

12.

▶ Describe Trapezoids

The quadrilaterals below are **trapezoids**.

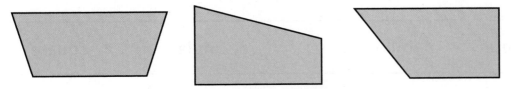

13. Write what you know about the **opposite sides** of a trapezoid.

14. Circle the quadrilaterals that are trapezoids.

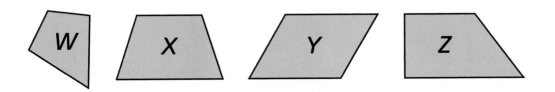

15. Explain why the figures you did not circle are not trapezoids.

Parallelograms, Rectangles, Squares, and Rhombuses

6-3 Class Activity

▶ Draw Parallelograms

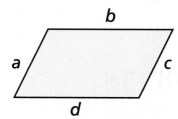

1. Write what you know about the opposite sides of a parallelogram.

2. Draw three different parallelograms.

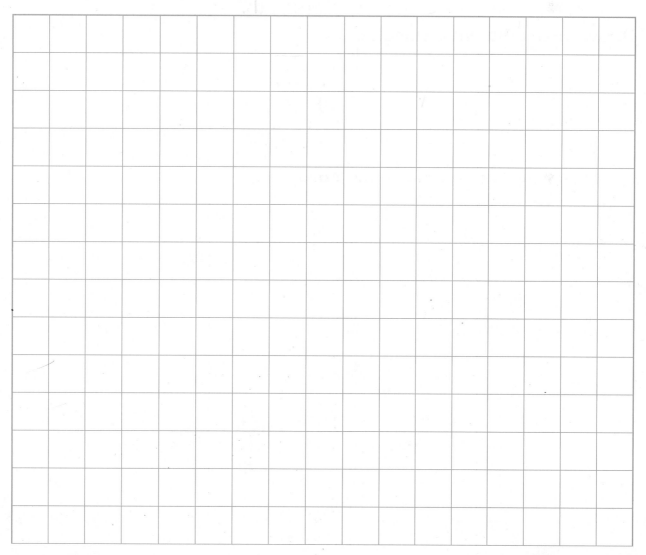

Draw Quadrilaterals

Use Activity Workbook page 168.

VOCABULARY
adjacent sides

▶ **Draw Rectangles**

3. Write everything you know about the opposite sides of a rectangle.

4. What do you know about the **adjacent sides** of a rectangle?

5. Draw three different rectangles.

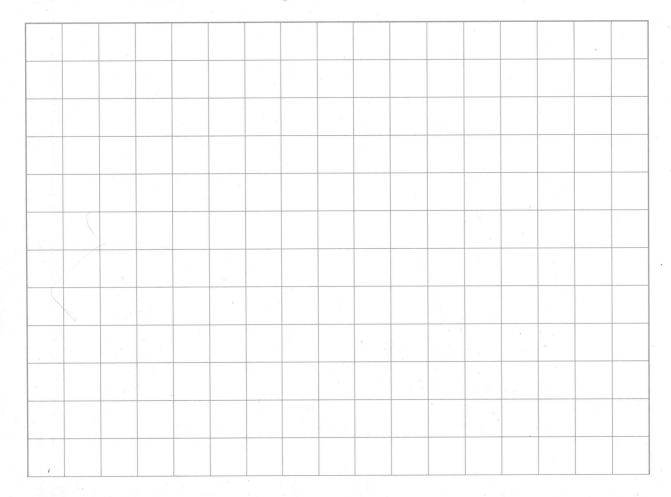

Draw Quadrilaterals

Use Activity
Workbook page 169.

▶ Draw Squares and Rhombuses

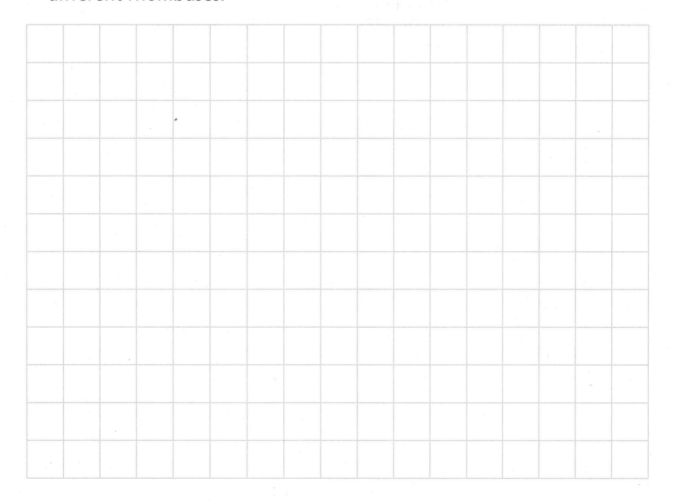

6. Write everything you know about squares.

7. Write all you know about rhombuses.

8. Draw two different squares and two different rhombuses.

Use Activity
Workbook page 170.

▶ **Draw Quadrilaterals That Are Not Squares, Rectangles, or Rhombuses**

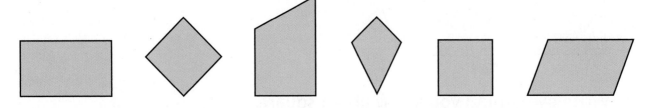

9. What is a quadrilateral?

10. Name all the quadrilaterals that have at least one pair of parallel sides.

11. Draw three different quadrilaterals that are not squares, rectangles, or rhombuses.

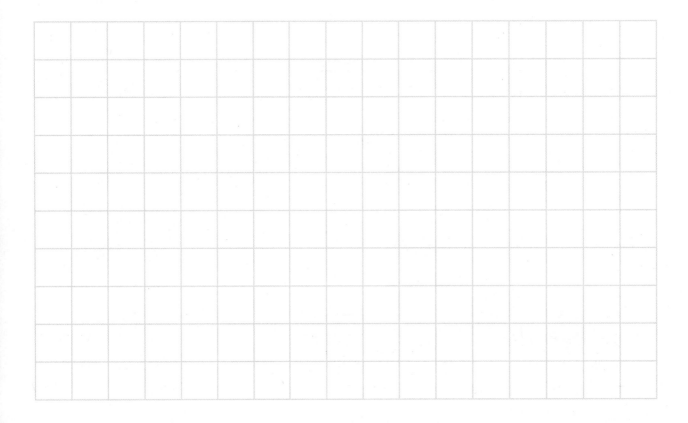

Draw Quadrilaterals

Use Activity Workbook page 171.

▶ Name Quadrilaterals

Place a check mark beside every name that describes the figure.

1.

- ☐ quadrilateral
- ☐ parallelogram
- ☐ rhombus
- ☐ rectangle
- ☐ square

2.

- ☐ quadrilateral
- ☐ parallelogram
- ☐ rhombus
- ☐ rectangle
- ☐ trapezoid

3.

- ☐ quadrilateral
- ☐ parallelogram
- ☐ rhombus
- ☐ rectangle
- ☐ square

4.

- ☐ quadrilateral
- ☐ parallelogram
- ☐ rhombus
- ☐ rectangle
- ☐ square

5.

- ☐ quadrilateral
- ☐ parallelogram
- ☐ rhombus
- ☐ rectangle
- ☐ square

6.

- ☐ quadrilateral
- ☐ parallelogram
- ☐ rhombus
- ☐ rectangle
- ☐ square

7.

- ☐ quadrilateral
- ☐ parallelogram
- ☐ rhombus
- ☐ rectangle
- ☐ square

8.

- ☐ quadrilateral
- ☐ parallelogram
- ☐ rhombus
- ☐ rectangle
- ☐ square

9.

- ☐ quadrilateral
- ☐ parallelogram
- ☐ rhombus
- ☐ rectangle
- ☐ square

Use Activity Workbook page 172.

▶ Analyze Quadrilaterals

10. For each figure, put Xs under the descriptions that are always true.

	Four sides	Both pairs of opposite sides parallel	Both pairs of opposite sides the same length	Four right angles	All sides the same length
Quadrilateral					
Trapezoid					
Parallelogram					
Rhombus					
Rectangle					
Square					

Use the finished chart above to complete each statement.

11. Parallelograms have all the features of quadrilaterals *plus*

12. Rectangles have all the features of parallelograms *plus*

13. Squares have all the features of quadrilaterals *plus*

14. Trapezoids have all the features of quadrilaterals *plus*

Classify Quadrilaterals

Use Activity
Workbook page 173.

► **Draw Quadrilaterals from a Description**

Draw each figure.

15. Draw a quadrilateral that is *not* a parallelogram.

16. Draw a parallelogram that is *not* a rectangle.

17. Draw a rectangle that is *not* a square.

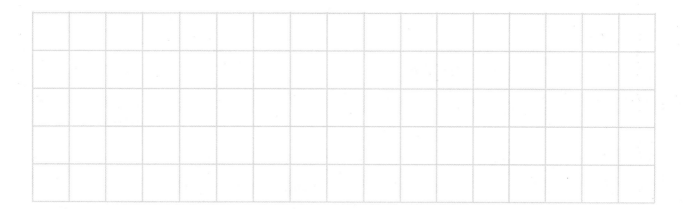

► **What's the Error?**

Dear Math Students,

Today I had to draw a quadrilateral with parallel sides that is not a rectangle, square, or rhombus. This is my drawing.

Is my drawing correct? If not, please help me understand why it is wrong.

Your friend,
Puzzled Penguin

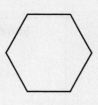

18. Write an answer to Puzzled Penguin.

Use the figures from Activity Workbook page 175.

▶ Sort and Classify Quadrilaterals

Use the category diagram to sort the figures you cut out from Student Book page 315A. Write the letter of the figure in the diagram to record your work.

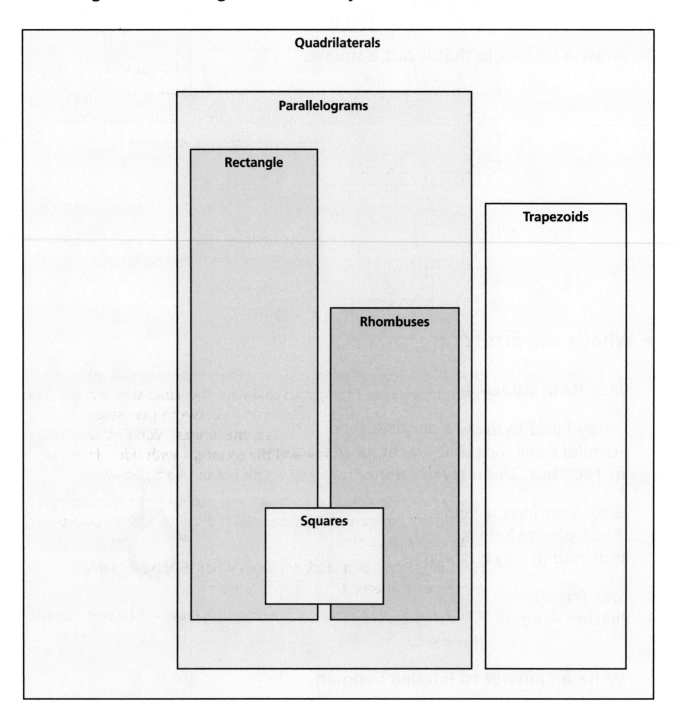

Classify Quadrilaterals

Dear Family,

Your child is currently learning about perimeter and area. Students begin to investigate the area of a rectangle by counting the number of square units inside the figure. Students also find the perimeter of a rectangle by counting linear units around the outside of the figure.

Students develop methods to find the perimeter and area of a rectangle, as shown below.

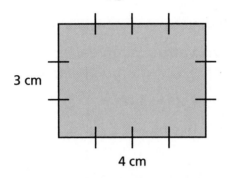

3 cm

4 cm

Perimeter = distance around the rectangle

Perimeter = side length + side length + side length + side length

$P = 4 \text{ cm} + 3 \text{ cm} + 4 \text{ cm} + 3 \text{ cm}$

$P = 14 \text{ cm}$

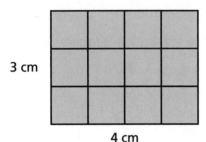

3 cm

4 cm

Area = square units inside the rectangle

Area = side length × side length

$A = 4 \text{ cm} \times 3 \text{ cm}$

$A = 12 \text{ sq cm}$

Students draw rectangles that have the same perimeter but different areas and rectangles that have the same area but different perimeters. They discover relationships between perimeter and area, such as that for a given area, the longest, skinniest rectangle has the greatest perimeter and the rectangle with sides closest to the same length or the same length has the least perimeter.

Share with your family the Family Letter on Activity Workbook page 177.

Students create shapes with tangrams, explore area relationships among the tangram shapes, and use the shapes as improvised units to measure area.

Throughout the unit students apply what they have learned about perimeter and area to real world problems.

If you have any questions or comments, please call or write to me.

Thank you.

Sincerely,
Your child's teacher

COMMON CORE This unit includes the Common Core Standards for Mathematical Content for Measurement and Data 3.MD.5, 3.MD.5a, 3.MD.5b, 3.MD.6, 3.MD.7, 3.MD.7a, 3.MD.7b, 3.MD.8, and all Mathematical Practices.

Estimada familia:

Su niño está aprendiendo acerca de perímetro y área. Los estudiantes comenzarán a investigar el área de un rectángulo contando las unidades cuadradas que caben en la figura. También hallarán el perímetro de un rectángulo contando las unidades lineales alrededor de la figura.

Los estudiantes desarrollarán métodos para hallar el perímetro y el área de un rectángulo, como se muestra a continuación.

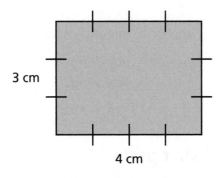

Perímetro = distancia alrededor del rectángulo

Perímetro = largo del lado + largo del lado + largo del lado + largo del lado

$P = 4 \text{ cm} + 3 \text{ cm} + 4 \text{ cm} + 3 \text{ cm}$

$P = 14 \text{ cm}$

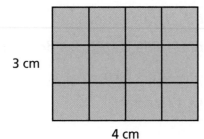

Área = unidades cuadradas dentro del rectángulo

Área = largo del lado × largo del lado

$A = 4 \text{ cm} \times 3 \text{ cm}$

$A = 12 \text{ cm cuad}$

Los estudiantes dibujarán rectángulos con el mismo perímetro pero diferentes áreas y rectángulos con la misma área pero diferentes perímetros. Descubrirán cómo se relacionan el perímetro y el área, por ejemplo, para un área determinada, el rectángulo más largo y angosto tiene el perímetro mayor y el rectángulo con lados de igual o casi igual longitud, tiene el perímetro menor.

Los estudiantes crearán figuras con tangramas, explorarán la relación entre el área de esas figuras y las usarán como medidas improvisadas para medir área.

Durante esta unidad los estudiantes aplicarán a problemas cotidianos lo que han aprendido acerca del perímetro y el área.

Si tiene alguna duda o algún comentario, por favor comuníquese conmigo.

Atentamente,
El maestro de su niño

Muestra a tu familia la Carta a la familia de la página 178 del Cuaderno de actividades y trabajo.

COMMON CORE — Esta unidad incluye los Common Core Standards for Mathematical Content for Measurement and Data 3.MD.5, 3.MD.5a, 3.MD.5b, 3.MD.6, 3.MD.7, 3.MD.7a, 3.MD.7b, 3.MD.8, and all Mathematical Practices.

Use Activity
Workbook page 179.

VOCABULARY
perimeter
area
unit square

► **Recognize Perimeter and Area**

**On this page, the dots on the dot paper are
1 cm apart. Use the rectangle for Exercises 1–4.**

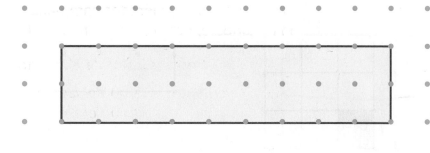

1. What part of the rectangle is its **perimeter**?

2. What part of the rectangle is its **area**?

3. Find the perimeter. Draw tick marks to help.

4. Find the area. Draw **unit squares** to help.

5. Draw a rectangle 5 cm long and 3 cm wide on the dot paper. Find the perimeter and area.

6. Explain how you found the area of the rectangle in Exercise 5.

Perimeter

Area

Use Activity Workbook page 180.

▶ Find Perimeter and Area

Find the perimeter and area of each figure.
Remember to include the correct units in your answers.

7.   perimeter   area

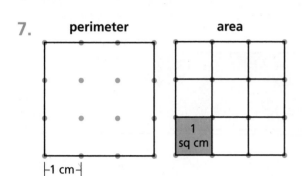

├─1 cm─┤

Perimeter = ▣

Area = ▣

8.

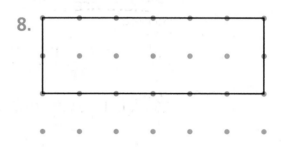

Perimeter = ▣

Area = ▣

9.

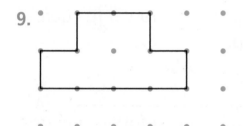

Perimeter = ▣

Area = ▣

10.

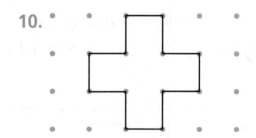

Perimeter = ▣

Area = ▣

11.

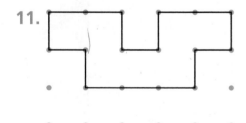

Perimeter = ▣

Area = ▣

12.

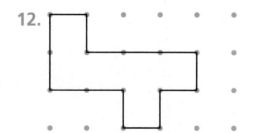

Perimeter = ▣

Area = ▣

Use the unit squares from Activity Workbook page 181.

▶ Tile a Rectangle

13. Use the 1-inch unit squares from page 319A to cover the rectangle below.

14. Check whether there are any gaps between the unit squares.

15. Check whether any unit squares overlap.

16. Draw lines to show the unit squares. The number of unit squares is the area in square inches. What is the area?

17. Use an inch ruler to measure the side lengths of the rectangle. Label the length and the width.

18. Write a multiplication equation to show the area.

Use the unit squares from Activity Workbook page 181.

▶ Tile a Rectangle (continued)

Cover each rectangle with 1-inch unit squares. Count the squares to find the area. Then write an equation to show the area.

19.

The area is _____   The equation is _____

20.

The area is _____   The equation is _____

21. How many 1-inch unit squares are needed to cover a rectangle that is 7 inches long and 4 inches wide?

22. What is the area of a rectangle that is 7 inches long and 4 inches wide?

Use Activity
Workbook page 185.

▶ Write Different Equations for Area

1. Use the drawings. Show two ways to find the area of a rectangle that is 10 units long and 6 units wide.

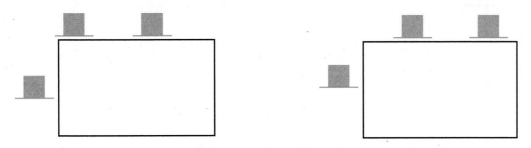

2. Write equations for your two rectangle drawings.

3. Suppose the rectangle is 10 feet long and 6 feet wide. What is its area?

4. Suppose the rectangle is 10 meters long and 6 meters wide. What is its area?

5. Use drawings and write equations to show two ways to find the area of a rectangle that is 9 yards long and 5 yards wide.

Show your work on your paper or in your journal.

▶ Rectangle Equations and Drawings

Write an equation for each rectangle.

6.
```
    3  +  5
 ┌─────┬────────┐
4│     │        │
 └─────┴────────┘
```

7.
```
   2 + 4
 ┌────┬────┐
5│    │    │
 │    │    │
 └────┴────┘
```

8.
```
    3  +    6
 ┌────┬─────────┐
3│    │         │
 └────┴─────────┘
```

9.
```
    4  +   4
 ┌──────┬──────┐
4│      │      │
 │      │      │
 └──────┴──────┘
```

Draw a rectangle for each equation.

10. $(3 \times 3) + (3 \times 5) = 3 \times 8$

11. $(4 \times 5) + (4 \times 3) = 4 \times 8$

12. $(5 \times 3) + (5 \times 6) = 5 \times 9$

13. $(4 \times 6) + (4 \times 4) = 4 \times 10$

▶ Find Unknown Side Lengths

Find the unknown side length in each diagram.

14.
```
        8 cm
 ┌──────────────────┐
?│                  │
 └──────────────────┘
```
Area = 72 sq cm

15.

```
        12 cm
 ┌──────────────────┐
?│                  │
 └──────────────────┘
```
Perimeter = 38 cm

16.
```
          ?
 ┌──────────────────┐
24│                 │
 └──────────────────┘
```
Perimeter = 64 cm

17.
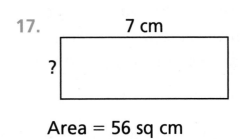
```
        7 cm
 ┌──────────────────┐
?│                  │
 └──────────────────┘
```
Area = 56 sq cm

18.
```
        30 cm
 ┌──────────────────┐
?│                  │
 └──────────────────┘
```
Perimeter = 72 cm

19.
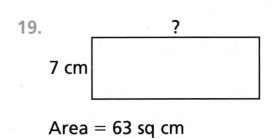
```
          ?
 ┌──────────────────┐
7 cm│                │
 └──────────────────┘
```
Area = 63 sq cm

20.
```
        7 cm
 ┌──────────────────┐
?│                  │
 └──────────────────┘
```
Area = 28 sq cm

21.
```
        7 cm
 ┌──────────────────┐
?│                  │
 └──────────────────┘
```
Perimeter = 28 cm

Show your work
on your paper or
in your journal.

▶ Unknown Side Length Problems

Solve. Draw a rectangle to represent the situation.

22. Alexander and his grandfather are tiling their rectangular kitchen floor. They need to use 42 tiles. They are making rows of 7 tiles. How many rows do they make?

23. Tilly and her mom made a rectangular dog run. They used 12 one-yard long pieces of fencing. They put 2 pieces of fencing on one side. How many pieces did they put on the next side?

24. Martha is making a quilt. She has 63 squares ready to sew together. She wants the quilt to be 9 rows long. How many squares will be in each row?

25. Rick and Roger are painting a mural made up of different sizes of rectangles, with no gaps or overlaps of the rectangles. They have enough paint to cover 15 square yards. They want the mural to be 3 yards long. How wide can the mural be?

26. Mr. Baker wants to use all of a 48-inch strip of oak trim for a box he plans to make. He wants the box to be 14 inches wide. How long will the box be?

► **Compare Rectangles with the Same Perimeter**

Complete.

Your teacher will give you centimeter grid paper. Write your answers on Activity Workbook page 187.

1. On a centimeter dot grid, draw all possible rectangles with a perimeter of 12 cm and sides whose lengths are whole centimeters. Label the lengths of two adjacent sides of each rectangle.

2. Find and label the area of each rectangle. In the table, record the lengths of the adjacent sides and the area of each rectangle.

3. Compare the shapes of the rectangles with the least and greatest areas.

Rectangles with Perimeter 12 cm	
Lengths of Two Adjacent Sides	Area

4. On a centimeter dot grid, draw all possible rectangles with a perimeter of 22 cm and sides whose lengths are whole centimeters. Label the lengths of two adjacent sides of each rectangle.

5. Find and label the area of each rectangle. In the table, record the lengths of the adjacent sides and the area of each rectangle.

6. Compare the shapes of the rectangles with the least and greatest areas.

Rectangles with Perimeter 22 cm	
Lengths of Two Adjacent Sides	Area

Your teacher will give you centimeter dot paper. Write your answers on Activity Workbook page 188.

▶ **Compare Rectangles with the Same Area**

Complete.

7. On a centimeter dot grid, draw all possible rectangles with an area of 12 sq cm and sides whose lengths are whole centimeters. Label the lengths of two adjacent sides of each rectangle.

8. Find and label the perimeter of each rectangle. In the table, record the lengths of the adjacent sides and the perimeter of each rectangle.

9. Compare the shapes of the rectangles with the least and greatest perimeter.

| Rectangles with Area 12 sq cm ||
Lengths of Two Adjacent Sides	Perimeter

10. On a centimeter dot grid, draw all possible rectangles with an area of 18 sq cm and sides whose lengths are whole centimeters. Label the lengths of two adjacent sides of each rectangle.

11. Find and label the perimeter of each rectangle. In the table, record the lengths of the adjacent sides and the perimeter of each rectangle.

| Rectangles with Area 18 sq cm ||
Lengths of Two Adjacent Sides	Perimeter

12. Compare the shapes of the rectangles with the least and greatest perimeter.

Compare Areas and Perimeters

Use Activity
Workbook page 189.

▶ Find Area by Decomposing into Rectangles

Decompose each figure into rectangles.
Then find the area of the figure.

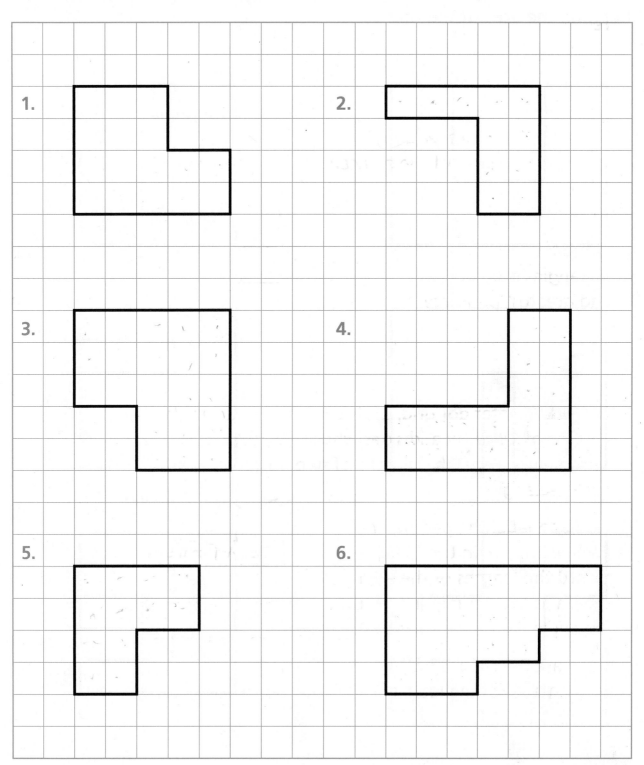

1.

2.

3.

4.

5.

6.

Use Activity
Workbook page 190.

► Find Area by Decomposing into Rectangles (continued)

**Decompose each figure into rectangles.
Then find the area of the figure.**

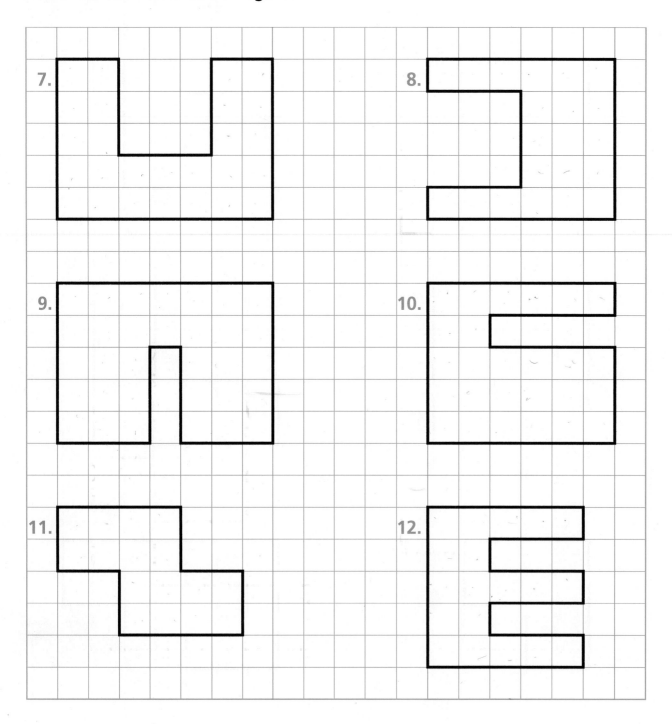

Area of Rectilinear Figures

Use Activity Workbook page 191.

► Find Area by Decomposing into Rectangles (continued)

Decompose each figure into rectangles. Then find the area of the figure.

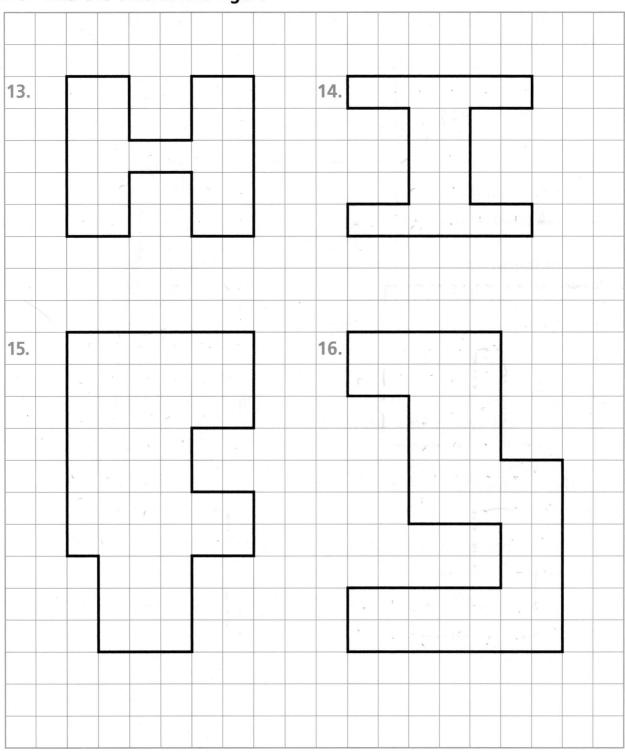

13.

14.

15.

16.

► **What's the Error?**

Dear Math Students,

Today my teacher asked me to find the area of a figure.
I knew that I could decompose the figure into rectangles.
This is what I did.

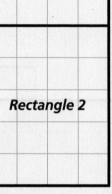

Rectangle 1

Rectangle 2

Area of Rectangle 1:
3 x 6 = 18 square units

Area of Rectangle 2:
5 x 4 = 20 square units

Area of Figure:
18 + 20 = 38 square units

Is my work correct? If not, please correct my work and tell
me what I did wrong. How do you know my answer is wrong?

Your friend,
Puzzled Penguin

17. Write an answer to Puzzled Penguin.

▶ **Solve Perimeter and Area Problems**

Show your work on your paper or in your journal.

Solve. Circle whether you need to find a perimeter, an area, or an unknown side length. Draw a diagram to represent each situation.

1. The dimensions of a rectangular picture frame are 9 inches and 6 inches. What is the area of a picture that would fit in the frame?

   Perimeter   Area   Side Length

2. A garden has the shape of a hexagon. Each side of the garden is 5 feet long. How much fence is needed to go around the garden?

   Perimeter   Area   Side Length

3. The length of a water slide is 9 yards. The slide is 2 yards wide. How much of the surface of the slide must be covered with water?

   Perimeter   Area   Side Length

4. Mr. Schmidt is installing 32 cubbies in the hallway. He puts 8 cubbies in each row. How many rows of cubbies can he make?

   Perimeter   Area   Side Length

Show your work on your paper or in your journal.

▶ Solve Perimeter and Area Problems (continued)

Solve. Circle whether you need to find a perimeter, an area, or an unknown side length. Draw a diagram to represent each situation.

5. The floor of a delivery van has an area of 56 square feet and is 8 feet long. How many rows of 8 boxes that measure 1 foot by 1 foot can be put in the delivery van?

   Perimeter   Area   Side Length

6. Zack is planning to make a flower garden. He has 24 one-yard sections of fence that he plans to place around the garden. He wants the garden to be as long as possible. What is the longest length he can use for the garden? How wide will the garden be?

   Perimeter   Area   Side Length

7. A spa is 9 yards long and 7 yards wide. A locker room 8 yards long and 6 yards wide is at one end of the spa. How much floor space do the spa and the locker room take up?

   Perimeter   Area   Side Length

8. Rosa's dog Sparky is 24 inches long. One side of Sparky's doghouse is 36 inches long and the other side is twice as long as Sparky. What is the distance around Sparky's doghouse?

   Perimeter   Area   Side Length

▶ Solve Perimeter and Area Problems (continued)

Solve. Circle whether you need to find a perimeter, an area, or an unknown side length. Draw a diagram to represent each situation.

Show your work on your paper or in your journal.

9. Joanne made 16 fruit bars in a square pan. The fruit bars are 2 inches by 2 inches. What are the dimensions of the pan she used to bake the fruit bars?

   Perimeter   Area   Side Length

10. A scout troop is making triangular pennants for their tents. Two sides of each pennant are 2 feet long and the third side is 1 foot long. How much binding tape is needed to go around 4 pennants?

    Perimeter   Area   Side Length

11. A rectangular quilt is 5 feet wide and 7 feet long. How many feet of lace are needed to cover the edges of the quilt?

    Perimeter   Area   Side Length

12. Amy has a piece of fleece fabric that is 4 feet wide and 6 feet long. How many squares of fleece fabric that are 1 foot wide and 1 foot long can she cut from the fabric?

    Perimeter   Area   Side Length

Show your work on your paper or in your journal.

▶ Solve Perimeter and Area Problems (continued)

Solve. Circle whether you need to find a perimeter, an area, or an unknown side length. Draw a diagram to represent each situation.

13. Leighanne has 23 tiles with dimensions of 1 foot by 1 foot. She wants to tile a hallway that is 8 feet long and 3 feet wide. Does she have enough tiles? If not, how many more does she need?

    Perimeter   Area   Side Length

14. Mrs. Brown has 48 one-foot pieces of garden fence for her new vegetable garden. She wants to have as much room as possible to plant the vegetables. What dimensions should she use for the garden?

    Perimeter   Area   Side Length

15. Martha has 27 quilt patches with animals and 27 patches with flowers. She wants her quilt to have rows of 6 patches. How many rows will the quilt have?

    Perimeter   Area   Side Length

16. A park in the shape of a triangle has a 20-mile bike path going along the sides. Donald rode 6 miles on the first side and 8 miles on the second side. How long is the third side of the park?

    Perimeter   Area   Side Length

Use the tangram pieces from Activity Workbook page 193.

► **Solve Tangram Puzzles**

Use the tangram pieces from page 335A.

1. Make this bird. When you finish, draw lines to show how you placed the pieces.

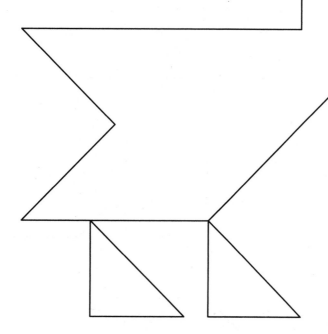

2. Make this rectangle. Draw lines to show how you placed the pieces. Hint: You do not need all the pieces.

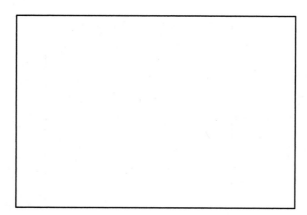

Use the tangram pieces from Activity Workbook page 193.

► Solve Tangram Puzzles (continued)

Use the tangram pieces. Draw lines to show how you placed the pieces.

3. Make this boat.

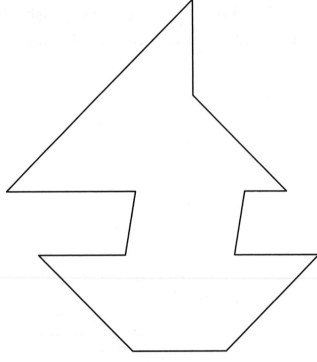

4. Make this tree.

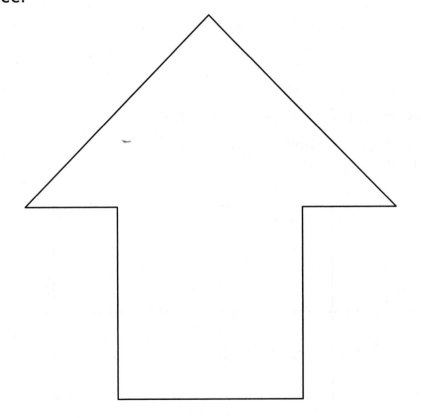

Tangram Shapes and Area

Use the tangram pieces from Activity Workbook page 193.

▶ Use Tangram Pieces to Find Area

5. Use the seven tangram pieces. Cover this rectangle.

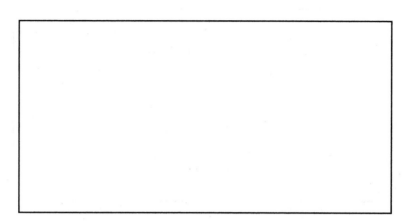

6. What is the area of the rectangle?

7. Use any tangram pieces. Cover this rectangle.

8. What is the area of the rectangle?

Use the tangram pieces from Activity Workbook page 193.

► Use Tangram Pieces to Find Area (continued)

Use any tangram pieces. Cover each rectangle.

9.

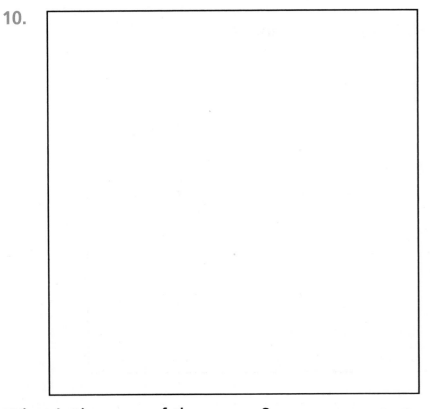

What is the area of the rectangle?

10.

What is the area of the square?

Tangram Shapes and Area

Use the tangram pieces from Activity Workbook page 193.

▶ Use Tangram Pieces to Find Area (continued)

Use any tangram pieces. Cover each figure.

11.

12.

What is the area of the square?

What is the area of the rectangle?

13.

What is the area of the figure?

6-10

Class Activity

Use the tangram pieces from Activity Workbook page 193.

▶ **Use Tangram Pieces to Find Area (continued)**

Use any tangram pieces. Cover each figure.

14.

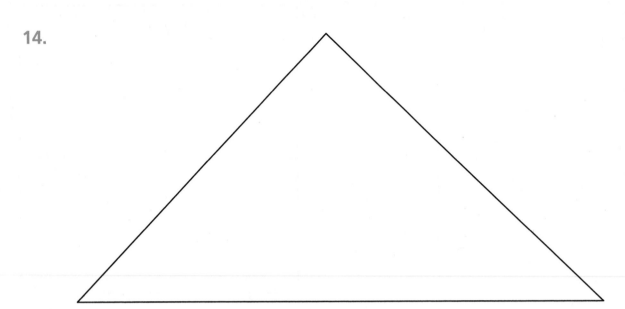

What is the area of the triangle?

15.

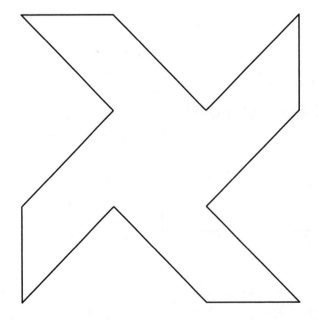

What is the area of the figure?

Tangram Shapes and Area

Use Activity
Workbook page 201.

▶ Math and Gardening

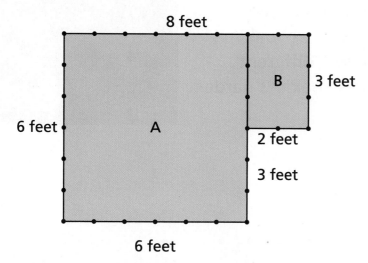

Look at the drawing of Yoakim's garden.
It is divided into two quadrilaterals.

1. What is the perimeter of part A?

   What is the perimeter of part B?

2. What is the perimeter of the combined garden?

3. Will Yoakim need more fencing to enclose the two parts of his garden separately or to enclose the combined garden?

4. What is the area of part A?

   What is the area of part B?

5. What is the area of the combined garden?

6. How does the total area of the two parts of the garden compare to the area of the combined garden?

Use Activity Workbook page 202.

▶ Design a Garden

Use the dot paper below to draw a different garden that has the same perimeter as Yoakim's combined garden. Beside it, draw a different garden that has the same area as Yoakim's garden.

⊢1 ft⊣

7. What is the area of your garden that has the same perimeter as Yoakim's garden?

8. What is the perimeter of your garden that has the same area as Yoakim's garden?

9. Use the centimeter dot paper at the right to draw separate areas within a garden where you would plant corn, beans, and tomatoes.

   The area for corn is 12 square feet.
   The area for beans is 25 square feet.
   The area for tomatoes is 20 square feet.

Focus on Mathematical Practices

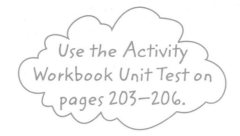
Use the Activity Workbook Unit Test on pages 203–206.

VOCABULARY
quadrilateral
rectangle
rhombus
area
perimeter

▶ Vocabulary

Choose the best word from the box.

1. A _____?_____ is a four-sided figure with 4 right angles. (Lesson 6-2)

2. The _____?_____ of a figure is the number of square units in the figure. (Lesson 6-5)

3. A _____?_____ is a parallelogram with all sides equal. (Lesson 6-2)

4. The _____?_____ of a figure is the distance around it. (Lesson 6-5)

▶ Concepts and Skills

5. To which larger category do parallelograms, rectangles, squares, rhombuses, and trapezoids belong? Explain. (Lesson 6-4)

6. How is area measured? (Lesson 6-5)

7. Show all the ways you can use to find the area of the rectangle at the right. (Lessons 6-5, 6-6, 6-10)

3 in.

2 in.

Put a check mark beside every name that describes the figure. (Lessons 6-2, 6-3, 6-4)

8.

☐ quadrilateral

☐ not a quadrilateral

☐ rectangle

☐ square

9.

☐ quadrilateral

☐ not a quadrilateral

☐ rectangle

☐ square

10.

☐ quadrilateral

☐ not a quadrilateral

☐ rectangle

☐ square

11. This hexagon has been divided into triangles with equal areas. What part of the area of the hexagon is each triangle? (Lesson 6-10)

12. Draw a quadrilateral that is not a rectangle, square, or rhombus.

▶ **Problem Solving**

Solve.

13. Alejandra and her father tiled a bathroom floor. They used 48 tiles that measure 1 foot on a side. One side of the bathroom is 8 ft. How long is the other side? (Lesson 6-6)

14. Victor and his mother are making a rectangular corral for a pony. They used 66 feet of fencing. One side has 15 feet of fencing. How many feet of fencing does the other side have? (Lesson 6-6)

15. Dory is designing a sticker. She wants the sticker to have a perimeter of 14 cm. On the dot grid, draw all possible rectangles whose side lengths are whole centimeters. Label the lengths of the two adjacent sides of each rectangle. Label each rectangle with its area. (Lesson 6-7)

16. Jacob is designing a package label. He wants the area to be 12 square cm. On the dot grid, draw all possible rectangles whose side lengths are whole centimeters. Label the lengths of the two adjacent sides of each rectangle. Label each rectangle with its perimeter. (Lesson 6-7)

Solve.

17. Deshawn wants to build a fence around a rectangular garden. The garden is 5 yards long and 3 yards wide. The fence sections are 1 yard long. How many sections of fence does Deshawn need? What is the area of the garden? (Lessons 6-5, 6-9)

18. Liana wants to put a rope around two rectangular spaces next to each other in her yard for a garden. One space is 5 meters long and 6 meters wide. The other space is 3 meters long and 6 meters wide. How much rope does Liana need? What will be the area of the garden? (Lessons 6-5, 6-6, 6-9, 6-10)

Perimeter:

Area:

Perimeter:

Area:

19. A sandbox is in the shape of a pentagon. Each side is 5 feet long. How much wood is needed to go around the sandbox? (Lessons 6-2, 6-9)

20. **Extended Response** David and his mother are sewing a quilt together from squares 1 foot on a side. David's mother will sew a 3 feet by 5 feet section of the quilt. David will sew a 4 feet by 5 feet section of the quilt. What will the area of the quilt be? Explain how you found the answer. Draw a picture of the quilt to show your answer is correct. (Lessons 6-8, 6-11)

Dear Family,

In this unit, your child will be introduced to fractions. Students will build fractions from unit fractions and explore fractions as parts of a whole.

Unit Fraction

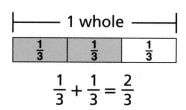

$$\frac{1}{3} + \frac{1}{3} = \frac{2}{3}$$

Fraction of a Whole

$\frac{3}{4}$ ← numerator
← denominator

Students will find equivalent fractions, and compare fractions with either the same denominator or the same numerator.

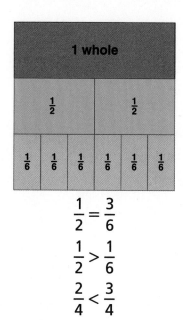

$$\frac{1}{2} = \frac{3}{6}$$

$$\frac{1}{2} > \frac{1}{6}$$

$$\frac{2}{4} < \frac{3}{4}$$

Share with your family the Family Letter on Activity Workbook page 207.

In this unit, your child will also solve real world problems using his or her understanding of fraction concepts.

Please call if you have any questions or comments.

Sincerely,
Your child's teacher

COMMON CORE

This unit includes the Common Core Standards for Mathematical Content for Numbers and Operations–Fractions, CC.3.NF.1, CC.3.NF.2a, CC.3.NF.2b, CC.3.NF.3a, CC.3.NF.3b, CC.3.NF.3c,CC.3.NF.3d; Geometry, CC.3.G.2 and for all Mathematical Practices.

Estimada familia:

En esta unidad, se le presentarán por primera vez las fracciones a su niño. Los estudiantes formarán fracciones con fracciones unitarias y explorarán las fracciones como partes de un entero.

Fracción unitaria

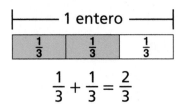

$$\frac{1}{3} + \frac{1}{3} = \frac{2}{3}$$

Fracción de un entero

$\frac{3}{4}$ ← numerador
← denominador

Los estudiantes hallarán fracciones equivalentes y compararán fracciones del mismo denominador o del mismo numerador.

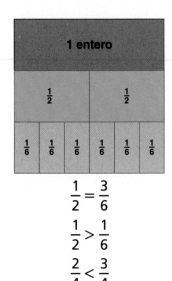

$$\frac{1}{2} = \frac{3}{6}$$

$$\frac{1}{2} > \frac{1}{6}$$

$$\frac{2}{4} < \frac{3}{4}$$

Muestra a tu familia la Carta a la familia de la página 208 del Cuaderno de actividades y trabajo.

En esta unidad, su niño también resolverá problemas cotidianos usando los conceptos que aprenda sobre fracciones.

Si tiene alguna duda o algún comentario, por favor comuníquese conmigo.

Atentamente,
El maestro de su niño

COMMON CORE

Esta unidad incluye los Common Core Standards for Mathematical Content for Numbers and Operations–Fractions, CC.3.NF.1, CC.3.NF.2a, CC.3.NF.2b, CC.3.NF.3a, CC.3.NF.3b, CC.3.NF.3c, CC.3.NF.3d; Geometry, CC.3.G.2 and for all Mathematical Practices.

Understand Fractions

Use the rectangles from Activity Workbook page 209.

▶ Explore Unit Fractions

Use your rectangles from page 349A to make the whole shape. Count the equal parts. What unit fraction of the whole shape is one of the rectangles?

1.

Number of equal parts _____   Unit fraction _____

2.

Number of equal parts _____   Unit fraction _____

3.

Number of equal parts _____   Unit fraction _____

Use the triangles from Activity Workbook page 209.

▶ Explore Unit Fractions (continued)

Use your triangles from page 349A to make a whole shape like the model shown. Count the equal parts in the whole. What unit fraction of the whole shape is the blue triangle?

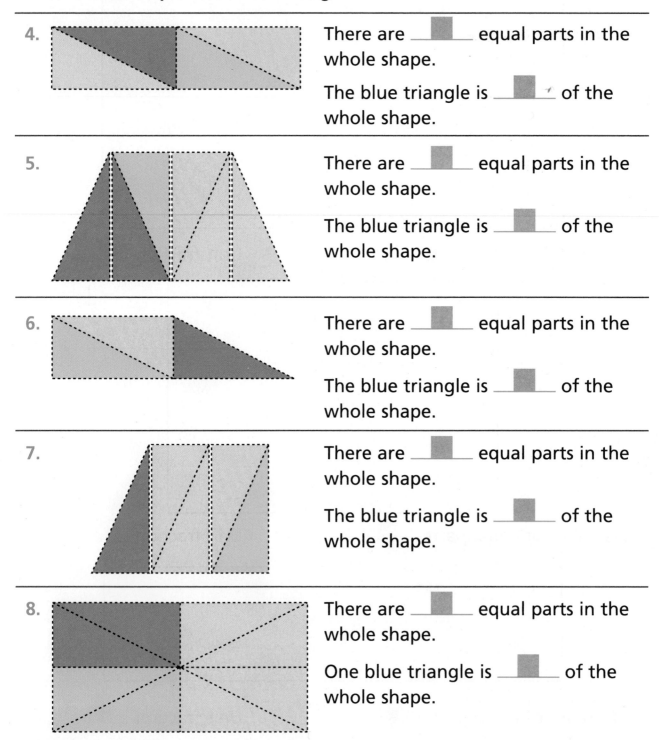

4.

There are _____ equal parts in the whole shape.

The blue triangle is _____ of the whole shape.

5.

There are _____ equal parts in the whole shape.

The blue triangle is _____ of the whole shape.

6.

There are _____ equal parts in the whole shape.

The blue triangle is _____ of the whole shape.

7.

There are _____ equal parts in the whole shape.

The blue triangle is _____ of the whole shape.

8.

There are _____ equal parts in the whole shape.

One blue triangle is _____ of the whole shape.

Use Activity Workbook page 211.

VOCABULARY
fraction   denominator
numerator   unit fraction

▶ Unit Fractions and Fraction Bars

You can represent a **fraction** with a fraction bar. The **denominator** tells how many equal parts the whole is divided into. The **numerator** tells how many equal parts you are talking about.

1 whole

$\dfrac{1}{3}$ ← numerator
← denominator

Shade 1 part.

A **unit fraction** has a numerator of 1. Shade the rest of the fraction bars at the right below to represent unit fractions. What patterns do you see?

1 whole → Shade 1 whole.   1   one

Divide the whole into 2 equal parts. → Shade 1 part. $\dfrac{1}{2}$ one half

Divide the whole into 3 equal parts. → Shade 1 part. $\dfrac{1}{3}$ one third

Divide the whole into 4 equal parts. → Shade 1 part. $\dfrac{1}{4}$ one fourth

Divide the whole into 5 equal parts. → Shade 1 part. $\dfrac{1}{5}$ one fifth

Divide the whole into 6 equal parts. → Shade 1 part. $\dfrac{1}{6}$ one sixth

Divide the whole into 7 equal parts. → Shade 1 part. $\dfrac{1}{7}$ one seventh

Divide the whole into 8 equal parts. → Shade 1 part. $\dfrac{1}{8}$ one eighth

Use Activity
Workbook page 212.

► Build Fractions from Unit Fractions

Write the unit fractions for each whole. Next, shade the correct number of parts. Then show each shaded fraction as a sum of unit fractions.

9. → Shade 2 parts.
Divide the whole into 5 equal parts.

$$\frac{1}{5} + \frac{1}{5} + \frac{1}{5} + \frac{1}{5} + \frac{1}{5}$$ $$\frac{1}{5} + \frac{1}{5} = \frac{2}{5}$$

10. → Shade 2 parts.
Divide the whole into 3 equal parts.

11. → Shade 5 parts.
Divide the whole into 7 equal parts.

12. → Shade 7 parts.
Divide the whole into 8 equal parts.

13. → Shade 3 parts.
Divide the whole into 6 equal parts.

14. → Shade 8 parts.
Divide the whole into 8 equal parts.

Understand Fractions

Use Activity
Workbook page 213.

► Use Fraction Bars

Shade each fraction bar to show the fraction.
First, divide the fraction bar into the correct unit fractions.

1. $\frac{1}{6}$ ├──────────── 1 whole ────────────┤

2. $\frac{2}{3}$ ├──────────── 1 whole ────────────┤

3. $\frac{7}{8}$ ├──────────── 1 whole ────────────┤

4. $\frac{2}{4}$ ├──────────── 1 whole ────────────┤

5. $\frac{5}{6}$ ├──────────── 1 whole ────────────┤

6. $\frac{3}{8}$ ├──────────── 1 whole ────────────┤

7-2

Class Activity

Use Activity
Workbook page 214.

▶ **Use Number Lines**

Mark each number line to show the fraction.
First, divide the number line into the correct unit fractions.

7. $\frac{1}{6}$

8. $\frac{2}{3}$

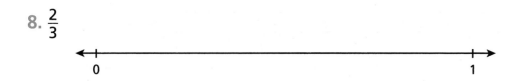

9. $\frac{7}{8}$

10. $\frac{2}{4}$

11. $\frac{5}{6}$

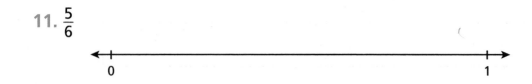

12. $\frac{3}{8}$

Model Fractions

Use Activity Workbook page 215.

▶ Locate Fractions Less Than 1

**Locate each fraction on the number line.
Draw more number lines if you need to.**

1. $\frac{1}{4}$ ◄—+————————————————+—►
                  0   1

2. $\frac{1}{8}$ ◄—+————————————————+—►
                  0   1

3. $\frac{2}{3}$ ◄—+————————————————+—►
                  0   1

4. $\frac{5}{6}$ ◄—+————————————————+—►
                  0   1

5. $\frac{1}{6}$ and $\frac{2}{3}$ ◄—+————————————————+—►
                                      0   1

6. $\frac{1}{3}$ and $\frac{5}{8}$ ◄—+————————————————+—►
                                      0   1

7. $\frac{1}{6}$ and $\frac{3}{4}$ ◄—+————————————————+—►
                                      0   1

Use Activity
Workbook page 216.

▶ Locate Fractions Greater Than 1

Locate each fraction on the number line.

8. $\frac{5}{4}$

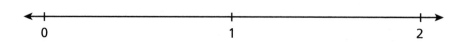

9. $\frac{8}{3}$

10. $\frac{5}{1}$

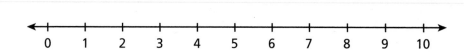

11. $\frac{8}{6}$

12. $\frac{6}{2}$

13. Explain how you located the fraction for one
of the Exercises from 8–12.

Use Activity
Workbook page 217.

► Find 1

Locate 1 on each number line.

14.

15.

16.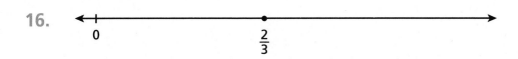

17.

18.

19. Explain how you located 1 for Exercise 17.

Locate Fractions on the Number Line **357**

Use Activity
Workbook page 218.

▶ **Find Fractions**

Locate each fraction on the number line.
Draw another number line if you need to.

20. $\frac{3}{4}$

21. $\frac{5}{6}$

22. $\frac{2}{3}$

23. $\frac{7}{4}$

24. $\frac{7}{8}$

25. $\frac{10}{8}$

Locate Fractions on the Number Line

▶ Compare Unit Fractions with Fraction Bars

The fraction bars are made up of unit fractions.
Look for patterns.

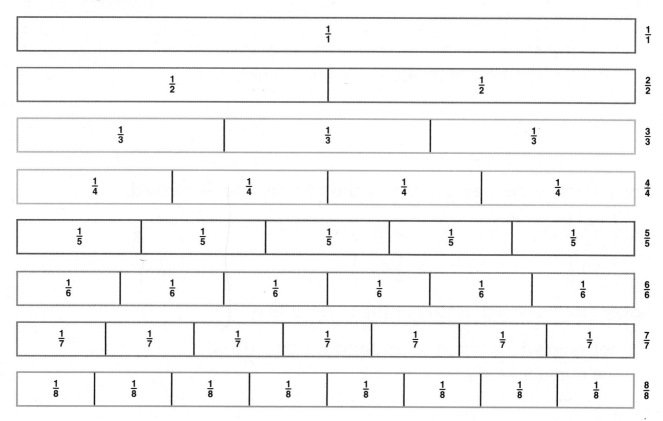

1. Describe two patterns that you see in the fraction bars.

Compare.

2. $\frac{1}{3}$ ⬤ $\frac{1}{7}$

3. $\frac{1}{3}$ ⬤ $\frac{1}{2}$

4. $\frac{1}{6}$ ⬤ $\frac{1}{7}$

▶ Compare Unit Fractions with Number Lines

The number line shows unit fractions.
Look for patterns in the number line.

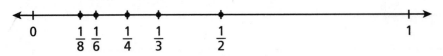

5. Describe a pattern that you see in the number line.

Compare. Use the fraction bars or the number line, if needed.

6. $\frac{1}{3}$ ⬤ $\frac{1}{8}$ 7. $\frac{1}{4}$ ⬤ $\frac{1}{2}$ 8. $\frac{1}{5}$ ⬤ $\frac{1}{8}$

9. $\frac{1}{2}$ ⬤ $\frac{1}{8}$ 10. $\frac{1}{4}$ ⬤ $\frac{1}{7}$ 11. $\frac{1}{6}$ ⬤ $\frac{1}{8}$

Solve. Use the fraction bars or the number line.

12. Between which two unit fractions would $\frac{1}{5}$ be on the number line?

13. Think about making a fraction bar for tenths.

  a. How many unit fractions would be in the fraction bar?

  b. How do you write the unit fraction?

14. **Predict** Can the fraction bars for any unit fractions with even denominators always be split into two equal parts? Explain your thinking.

Use the fraction circles from Activity Workbook page 219.

▶ **Compare Fractions**

Use these two circles as wholes.

Work with a partner. Use your fraction circles to compare fractions during the class activity.

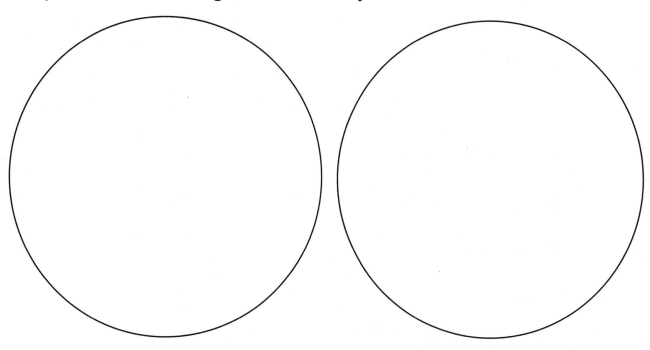

Record your work during the class activity.

1. $\frac{7}{8}$ ⬤ $\frac{5}{8}$ 2. $\frac{3}{6}$ ⬤ $\frac{5}{6}$

3. Explain how to compare two fractions that have the same denominator.

4. $\frac{3}{4}$ ⬤ $\frac{3}{8}$ 5. $\frac{5}{8}$ ⬤ $\frac{5}{6}$

6. Explain how to compare two fractions that have the same numerator.

► **Use Symbols to Compare Fractions**

Compare. Use <, >, or =.

7. $\frac{2}{2}$ ⬤ $\frac{2}{3}$

8. $\frac{1}{3}$ ⬤ $\frac{5}{3}$

9. $\frac{3}{2}$ ⬤ $\frac{3}{6}$

10. $\frac{5}{6}$ ⬤ $\frac{4}{6}$

11. $\frac{4}{6}$ ⬤ $\frac{5}{6}$

12. $\frac{3}{4}$ ⬤ $\frac{3}{8}$

13. $\frac{6}{3}$ ⬤ $\frac{5}{3}$

14. $\frac{8}{4}$ ⬤ $\frac{8}{7}$

15. $\frac{5}{6}$ ⬤ $\frac{5}{3}$

16. $\frac{8}{5}$ ⬤ $\frac{12}{5}$

17. $\frac{6}{5}$ ⬤ $\frac{6}{4}$

18. $\frac{2}{2}$ ⬤ $\frac{4}{4}$

19. $\frac{5}{8}$ ⬤ $\frac{3}{8}$

20. $\frac{7}{3}$ ⬤ $\frac{7}{6}$

21. $\frac{7}{8}$ ⬤ $\frac{3}{8}$

22. $\frac{9}{4}$ ⬤ $\frac{9}{8}$

23. $\frac{4}{4}$ ⬤ $\frac{6}{6}$

24. $\frac{12}{7}$ ⬤ $\frac{11}{7}$

25. $\frac{8}{6}$ ⬤ $\frac{8}{2}$

26. $\frac{8}{1}$ ⬤ $\frac{12}{1}$

► **What's the Error?**

Dear Math Students,

Today my teacher asked me to compare $\frac{3}{7}$ and $\frac{3}{9}$ and to explain my thinking.

I wrote $\frac{3}{7} = \frac{3}{9}$. My thinking is that both fractions have 3 unit fractions so they must be equal.

Is my work correct? If not, please correct my work and tell me what I did wrong. How do you know my answer is wrong?

Your friend,
Puzzled Penguin

27. Write an answer to Puzzled Penguin.

▶ Halves, Fourths, and Eighths

Two fractions are **equivalent fractions** if they name the same part of a whole.

Use your halves, fourths, and eighths strips to complete Exercises 1–4.

$\frac{1}{2}$				$\frac{1}{2}$			
$\frac{1}{4}$		$\frac{1}{4}$		$\frac{1}{4}$		$\frac{1}{4}$	
$\frac{1}{8}$	$\frac{1}{8}$	$\frac{1}{8}$	$\frac{1}{8}$	$\frac{1}{8}$	$\frac{1}{8}$	$\frac{1}{8}$	$\frac{1}{8}$

1. If you compare your halves strip and your fourths strip, you can see that 2 fourths are the same as 1 half.

   Complete these two equations:

   _____ fourths = 1 half

   $$\frac{}{4} = \frac{1}{2}$$

2. How many eighths are in one half? _____

   Complete these two equations:

   _____ eighths = 1 half

   $$\frac{}{8} = \frac{1}{2}$$

3. What are two fractions that are equivalent to $\frac{1}{2}$?

4. How many eighths are in one fourth? _____

   Complete these two equations:

   _____ eighths = 1 fourth

   $$\frac{}{8} = \frac{1}{4}$$

▶ Thirds and Sixths

Use your thirds and sixths strips to answer Exercises 5–6.

5. How many sixths are in one third? _____

Complete these two equations:

_____ sixths = 1 third

$$\frac{\boxed{}}{6} = \frac{1}{3}$$

6. How many sixths are in two thirds? _____

Complete these two equations:

_____ sixths = 2 thirds

$$\frac{\boxed{}}{6} = \frac{2}{3}$$

▶ What's the Error?

Dear Math Students,

Today my teacher asked me to name a fraction that is equivalent to $\frac{1}{2}$.

I wrote $\frac{2}{6} = \frac{1}{2}$

Is my answer correct? If not, please correct my work and tell me what I did wrong.

Your Friend,
Puzzled Penguin

7. Write an answer to Puzzled Penguin.

Use Activity
Workbook page 223.

VOCABULARY
equivalence chain

▶ Equivalent Fractions on Number Lines

1. Complete each number line. Show all fractions including each fraction for 1.

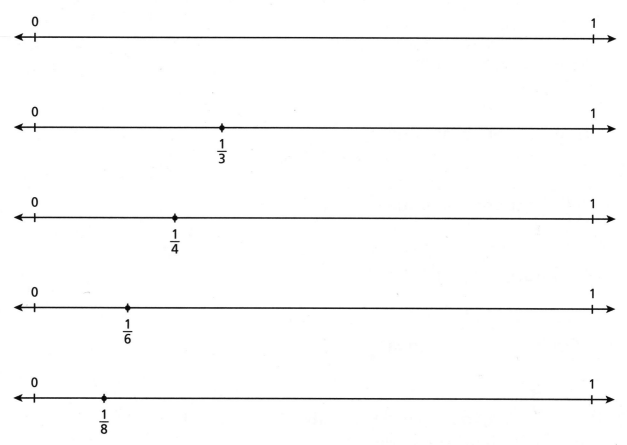

2. Write an equivalence chain with fractions that equal $\frac{2}{2}$.

3. Why are the fractions in the equivalence chain for $\frac{2}{2}$ equal?

4. Why does the length of unit fractions grow smaller as their denominators get larger?

▶ Equivalence Chains

Use your number lines from page 365 to write an equivalence chain.

5. With fractions that equal $\frac{1}{2}$

6. With fractions that equal $\frac{1}{3}$

7. With fractions that equal $\frac{2}{3}$

8. With fractions that equal $\frac{1}{4}$

9. With fractions that equal $\frac{3}{4}$

10. With fractions that equal $\frac{8}{8}$

Solve. Use what you have learned about equivalent fractions and about comparing fractions.

11. Jaime has $\frac{1}{2}$ dozen red marbles and $\frac{4}{8}$ dozen green marbles. Does he have more red or green marbles?

12. Nancy buys $\frac{3}{6}$ pound of walnuts. Sandra buys $\frac{3}{4}$ pound of almonds. Who buys more nuts?

13. Chin and Maya collected shells at the beach. They both used the same kind of basket. Chin collected $\frac{3}{4}$ basket and Maya collected $\frac{3}{3}$ basket. Who collected more shells?

► Solve Fraction Problems

Solve. Draw diagrams or number lines if you need to.

1. The shelves in Roger's bookcase are $\frac{7}{8}$ yard long. Latanya's bookcase has shelves that are $\frac{5}{8}$ yard long. Whose bookcase has longer shelves? How do you know?

2. Rosa buys $\frac{3}{4}$ pound of cheddar cheese. Lucy buys $\frac{3}{8}$ pound of goat cheese. Who buys more cheese? Explain your answer.

3. Martha baked $\frac{8}{4}$ dozen cranberry muffins. Vera baked $\frac{8}{6}$ dozen banana muffins. Who baked fewer muffins? How do you know?

4. Lester walks $\frac{3}{4}$ mile to school. Bert said that he walks farther because he walks $\frac{6}{8}$ mile to school. Is his statement correct? Explain your answer.

5. Jack's family has a pickup truck that weighs $\frac{9}{4}$ ton. Ruth's family has a car that weighs $\frac{9}{8}$ ton. Is the pickup truck or the car heavier? How do you know?

6. Rusty painted $\frac{5}{6}$ of a mural for the school hallway. Has he painted more than half of the mural? Explain your answer.
   Hint: Find an equivalent fraction in sixths for $\frac{1}{2}$.

▶ Solve Fraction Problems (continued)

Solve. Draw diagrams or number lines if it helps.

7. Pearl used $\frac{3}{3}$ yard of fabric to make a pillow.
   Julia made her pillow from $\frac{4}{4}$ yard of fabric.
   They both paid $5 a yard for their fabric.
   Who paid more for fabric? How do you know?

8. At Binata's Bakery, two different recipes are
   used for wheat bread. For a round loaf, $\frac{5}{2}$ cups of
   wheat flour is used. For a long loaf, $\frac{7}{2}$ cups of
   wheat flour is used. For which kind of bread is
   more wheat flour used? Explain your answer.

9. Deena's water bottle can hold a total of $\frac{2}{5}$ liter
   of water. John's water bottle can hold a total of
   $\frac{5}{2}$ liter of water. Whose water bottle holds
   more water? How do you know?

10. Andy, Lu, and Carlos have $\frac{3}{3}$, $\frac{3}{4}$, and $\frac{3}{6}$ dozen
    pencils, but not in that order. Andy has the fewest
    pencils and Lu has the most. How many pencils
    does each boy have? Explain.

Problem Solving with Fractions

▶ Math and Paper Folding

The art of paper folding began in China. Later, Japan's version of paper folding, called origami, became very popular. Origami sculptures are made from a flat sheet of square paper through folding and sculpting techniques without cuts or glue.

Complete.

1. Fold a square sheet of paper in half diagonally. What part of the square is each triangle?

2. Fold the paper in half again. What part of the square is each triangle?

3. Fold the paper in half again. Open the paper. What part of the square is each triangle?

4. Explain how you know the eight parts have the same area.

5. Fold four triangles to the center as shown on the right. What part of the square is each triangle? Explain how you know.

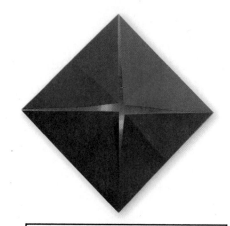

This basic origami fold is used for making many objects.

► **Math and Design**

Complete.

6. Fold a square sheet of paper in half three times.
   Open the paper. Choose two different colors.
   Color every other rectangle or triangle one color.
   Color the other rectangles or triangles the second color.

7. Write 3 equivalent fractions for the part of the square
   that is colored the same color.

8. Predict the number of shapes you would make
   if you folded the square 4 times. Explain.

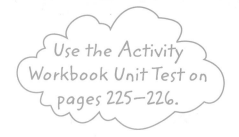
Use the Activity Workbook Unit Test on pages 225–226.

Use the Activity Workbook Unit Test on pages 225–226.

VOCABULARY
denominator
fraction
numerator
unit fraction

▶ Vocabulary

Choose the best word from the box.

1. A _____?_____ is a number that names one part of a whole and has a numerator of 1. (Lesson 7-1)

2. The bottom number in a fraction that tells how many equal parts the whole is divided into is called the _____?_____. (Lesson 7-1)

3. The top number in a fraction that tells how many of the equal parts you are talking about is called the _____?_____. (Lesson 7-1)

▶ Concepts and Skills

4. What are two ways you can tell if two fractions are equivalent? (Lessons 7-6, 7-7)

5. Why is $\frac{1}{2}$ of a pizza larger than $\frac{1}{4}$ of the same size pizza? (Lesson 7-4)

6. Write the unit fraction for the whole. Next, shade the correct number of parts. Then, show the shaded fraction as a sum of unit fractions. (Lessons 7-1, 7-2)

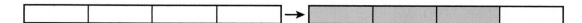

Divide the whole into 4 equal parts.

Mark the number line to show the fractions. First divide the number into correct unit fractions. (Lessons 7-2, 7-3, 7-8)

7. $\frac{1}{8}$ 8. $\frac{5}{8}$ 9. $\frac{8}{8}$ 10. $\frac{3}{4}$

0   1

Write an equivalence chain. Use your fraction strips or a number line if you need to. (Lessons 7-6, 7-7, 7-8)

11. With fractions that equal $\frac{1}{2}$

12. With fractions that equal $\frac{6}{6}$

Locate each fraction on the number line. (Lesson 7-3)

13. $\frac{3}{1}$ 14. $\frac{9}{6}$ 15. $\frac{4}{2}$

0   1   2   3

Compare. Use <, >, or =. (Lessons 7-4, 7-5)

16. $\frac{3}{8}$ ⬤ $\frac{5}{8}$ 17. $\frac{6}{3}$ ⬤ $\frac{6}{4}$ 18. $\frac{3}{3}$ ⬤ $\frac{2}{2}$

▶ **Problem Solving**

Solve. (Lessons 7-4, 7-5, 7-6, 7-7)

19. Diane's water bottle holds $\frac{5}{4}$ liter of water. Joe's holds $\frac{3}{4}$ liter of water. Whose water bottle holds more water? How do you know?

20. **Extended Response** Dan walks $\frac{5}{8}$ mile to school. Beth walks $\frac{3}{4}$ mile to school. Who walks farther? Explain your answer. Show you are correct using the circles.

Reference Tables

Table of Measures

Metric	Customary
Length/Area	

Length/Area

Metric	Customary
1 meter (m) = 10 decimeters (dm)	1 foot (ft) = 12 inches (in.)
1 meter (m) = 100 centimeters (cm)	1 yard = 3 feet (ft)
1 decimeter (dm) = 10 centimeters (cm)	1 mile (mi) = 5,280 feet (ft)
1 square centimeter = 1 cm²	1 square inch = 1 in²
A metric unit for measuring area. It is the area of a square that is one centimeter on each side.	A customary unit for measuring area. It is the area of a square that is one inch on each side.

Liquid Volume

Metric	Customary
1 liter (L) = 1,000 milliliters (mL)	1 tablespoon (tbsp) = $\frac{1}{2}$ fluid ounce (fl oz)
	1 cup (c) = 8 fluid ounces (fl oz)
	1 pint (pt) = 2 cups (c)
	1 quart (qt) = 2 pints (pt)
	1 gallon (gal) = 4 quarts (qt)

Table of Units of Time

Time

1 minute (min) = 60 seconds (sec)

1 hour (hr) = 60 minutes

1 day = 24 hours

1 week (wk) = 7 days

1 month, about 30 days

1 year (yr) = 12 months (mo)
or about 52 weeks

1 year = 365 days

1 leap year = 366 days

Properties of Operations

Associative Property of Addition

$(a + b) + c = a + (b + c)$ $(2 + 5) + 3 = 2 + (5 + 3)$

Commutative Property of Addition

$a + b = b + a$ $4 + 6 = 6 + 4$

Identity Property of Addition

$a + 0 = 0 + a = a$ $3 + 0 = 0 + 3 = 3$

Associative Property of Multiplication

$(a \cdot b) \cdot c = a \cdot (b \cdot c)$ $(3 \cdot 5) \cdot 7 = 3 \cdot (5 \cdot 7)$

Commutative Property of Multiplication

$a \cdot b = b \cdot a$ $6 \cdot 3 = 3 \cdot 6$

Identity Property of Multiplication

$a \cdot 1 = 1 \cdot a = a$ $8 \cdot 1 = 1 \cdot 8 = 8$

Zero Property of Multiplication

$a \cdot 0 = 0 \cdot a = 0$ $5 \cdot 0 = 0 \cdot 5 = 0$

Distributive Property of Multiplication over Addition

$a \cdot (b + c) = (a \cdot b) + (a \cdot c)$ $2 \cdot (4 + 3) = (2 \cdot 4) + (2 \cdot 3)$

Problem Types

Addition and Subtraction Problem Types

	Result Unknown	Change Unknown	Start Unknown
Add to	Aisha had 274 stamps in her collection. Then her grandfather gave her 65 stamps. How many stamps does she have now? *Situation and solution equation:*[1] $274 + 65 = s$	Aisha had 274 stamps in her collection. Then her grandfather gave her some stamps. Now she has 339 stamps. How many stamps did her grandfather give her? *Situation equation:* $274 + s = 339$ *Solution equation:* $s = 339 - 274$	Aisha had some stamps in her collection. Then her grandfather gave her 65 stamps. Now she has 339 stamps. How many stamps did she have to start? *Situation equation* $s + 65 = 339$ *Solution equation:* $s = 339 - 65$
Take from	A store had 750 bottles of water at the start of the day. During the day, the store sold 490 bottles. How many bottles did they have at the end of the day? *Situation and solution equation:* $750 - 490 = b$	A store had 750 bottles of water at the start of the day. The store had 260 bottles left at the end of the day. How many bottles did the store sell? *Situation equation:* $750 - b = 260$ *Solution equation:* $b = 750 - 260$	A store had a number of bottles of water at the start of the day. The store sold 490 bottles of water. At the end of the day 260 bottles were left. How many bottles did the store have to start with? *Situation equation:* $b - 490 = 260$ *Solution equation:* $b = 260 + 490$

[1]A situation equation represents the structure (action) in the problem situation. A solution equation shows the operation used to find the answer.

	Total Unknown	Addend Unknown	Other Addend Unknown
Put Together/ Take Apart	A clothing store has 375 shirts with short sleeves and 148 shirts with long sleeves. How many shirts does the store have in all? *Math drawing:* s 375 148 *Situation and solution equation:* $375 + 148 = s$	Of the 523 shirts in a clothing store, 375 have short sleeves. The rest have long sleeves. How many shirts have long sleeves? *Math drawing:* 523 375 s *Situation equation:* $523 = 375 + s$ *Solution equation:* $s = 523 - 375$	A clothing store has 523 shirts. Some have short sleeves and 148 have long sleeves. How many of the shirts have short sleeves? *Math drawing:* 523 s 148 *Situation equation* $523 = s + 148$ *Solution equation:* $s = 523 - 148$ •

© Houghton Mifflin Harcourt Publishing Company

Problem Types continued

Addition and Subtraction Problem Types (continued)

	Difference Unknown	Greater Unknown	Smaller Unknown
Compare	At a zoo, the female black bear weighs 175 pounds. The male black bear weighs 260 pounds. How much more does the male black bear weigh than the female black bear? At a zoo, the female black bear weighs 175 pounds. The male black bear weighs 260 pounds. How much less does the female black bear weigh than the male black bear? *Math drawing:* $\boxed{260}$ $\boxed{175}\ \bigcirc d$ *Situation equation:* $175 + d = 260$ or $d = 260 - 175$ *Solution equation:* $d = 260 - 175$	**Leading Language** At a zoo, the female black bear weighs 175 pounds. The male black bear weighs 85 pounds more than the female black bear. How much does the male black bear weigh? **Misleading Language** At a zoo, the female black bear weighs 175 pounds. The female black bear weighs 85 pounds less than the male black bear. How much does the male black bear weigh? *Math drawing:* $\boxed{m}$ $\boxed{175}\ \boxed{85}$ *Situation and solution equation:* $175 + 85 = m$	**Leading Language** At a zoo, the male black bear weighs 260 pounds. The female black bear weighs 85 pounds less than the male black bear. How much does the female black bear weigh? **Misleading Language** At a zoo, the male black bear weighs 260 pounds. The male black bear weighs 85 pounds more than the female black bear. How much does the female black bear weigh? *Math drawing:* $\boxed{260}$ $\boxed{f}\ \bigcirc 85$ *Situation equation* $f + 85 = 260$ or $f = 260 - 85$ *Solution equation:* $f = 260 - 85$

A comparison sentence can always be said in two ways. One way uses *more*, and the other uses *fewer* or *less*. Misleading language suggests the wrong operation. For example, it says *the female black bear weighs 85 pounds less than the male*, but you have to add 85 pounds to the female's weight to get the male's weight.

Multiplication and Division Problem Types

	Unknown Product	Group Size Unknown	Number of Groups Unknown
Equal Groups	A teacher bought 5 boxes of markers. There are 8 markers in each box. How many markers did the teacher buy?	A teacher bought 5 boxes of markers. She bought 40 markers in all. How many markers are in each box?	A teacher bought boxes of 8 markers. She bought 40 markers in all. How many boxes of markers did she buy?
	Math drawing:	*Math drawing:*	*Math drawing:*
	n $5\times$ ⑧ ⑧ ⑧ ⑧ ⑧	40 $5\times$ ⓝ ⓝ ⓝ ⓝ ⓝ	40 $n\times$ ⑧ ⑧ ⑧ ⑧ ⑧
	Situation and solution equation: $n = 5 \cdot 8$	*Situation equation:* $5 \cdot n = 40$ *Solution equation:* $n = 40 \div 5$	*Situation equation* $n \cdot 8 = 40$ *Solution equation:* $n = 40 \div 8$

Problem Types (continued)

	Unknown Product	Unknown Factor	Unknown Factor
Arrays	For the yearbook photo, the drama club stood in 3 rows of 7 students. How many students were in the photo in all? *Math drawing:* 7 3 ○○○○○○○ ○○○○○○○ ○○○○○○○ *Situation and solution equation:* $n = 3 \cdot 7$	For the yearbook photo, the 21 students in drama club, stood in 3 equal rows. How many students were in each row? *Math drawing:* n n Total: 21 n *Situation equation:* $3 \cdot n = 21$ *Solution equation:* $n = 21 \div 3$	For the yearbook photo, the 21 students in drama club, stood in rows of 7 students. How many rows were there? *Math drawing:* 7 7 Total: 21 7 *Situation equation* $n \cdot 7 = 21$ *Solution equation:* $n = 21 \div 7$
Area	The floor of the kitchen is 2 meters by 5 meters. What is the area of the floor? *Math drawing:* 5 2 [A] *Situation and solution equation:* $A = 5 \cdot 2$	The floor of the kitchen is 5 meters long. The area of the floor is 10 square meters. What is the width of the floor? *Math drawing:* 5 w [10] *Situation equation:* $5 \cdot w = 10$ *Solution equation:* $w = 10 \div 5$	The floor of the kitchen is 2 meters wide. The area of the floor is 10 square meters. What is the length of the floor? *Math drawing:* l 2 [10] *Situation equation* $l \cdot 2 = 10$ *Solution equation:* $l = 10 \div 2$

© Houghton Mifflin Harcourt Publishing Company

Vocabulary Activities

MathWord Power

▶ Word Review [PAIRS]

Work with a partner. Choose a word from a current unit or a review word from a previous unit. Use the word to complete one of the activities listed on the right. Then ask your partner if they have any edits to your work or questions about what you described. Repeat, having your partner choose a word.

Activities

▶ Give the meaning in words or gestures.

▶ Use the word in the sentence.

▶ Give another word that is related to the word in some way and explain the relationship.

▶ Crossword Puzzle [PAIRS] OR [INDIVIDUALS]

Create a crossword puzzle similar to the example below. Use vocabulary words from the unit. You can add other related words, too. Challenge your partner to solve the puzzle.

Across

1. _____ and subtraction are inverse operations.

2. To put amounts together

3. When you trade 10 ones for 1 ten, you _____.

4. The answer to an addition problem

Down

1. In 24 + 65 = 89, 24 is an _____.

3. A combination of the digits 0, 1, 2, 3, 4, 5, 6, 7, 8, and 9.

4. The operation that you can use to find out how much more one number is than another.

Vocabulary Activities (continued)

▶ Word Wall `PAIRS` OR `SMALL GROUPS`

With your teacher's permission, start a word wall in your classroom. As you work through each lesson, put the math vocabulary words on index cards and place them on the word wall. You can work with a partner or a small group choosing a word and giving the definition.

▶ Word Web `INDIVIDUALS`

Make a word web for a word or words you do not understand in a unit. Fill in the web with words or phrases that are related to the vocabulary word.

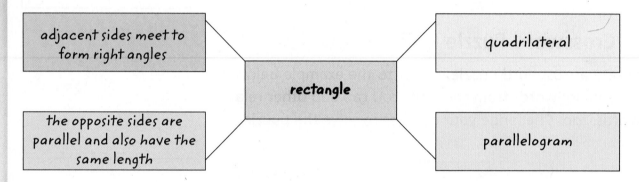

adjacent sides meet to form right angles

the opposite sides are parallel and also have the same length

rectangle

quadrilateral

parallelogram

▶ Alphabet Challenge `PAIRS` OR `INDIVIDUALS`

Take an alphabet challenge. Choose 3 letters from the alphabet. Think of three vocabulary words for each letter. Then write the definition or draw an example for each word.

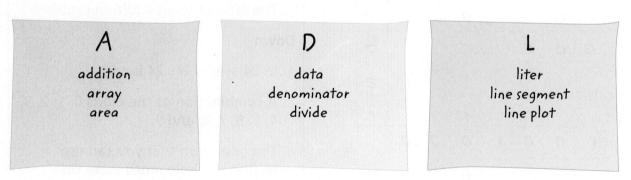

A
addition
array
area

D
data
denominator
divide

L
liter
line segment
line plot

▶ Concentration [PAIRS]

Write the vocabulary words and related words from a unit on index cards. Write the definitions on a different set of index cards. Mix up both sets of cards. Then place the cards facedown on a table in an array, for example, 3 by 3 or 3 by 4. Take turns turning over two cards. If one card is a word and one card is a definition that matches the word, take the pair. Continue until each word has been matched with its definition.

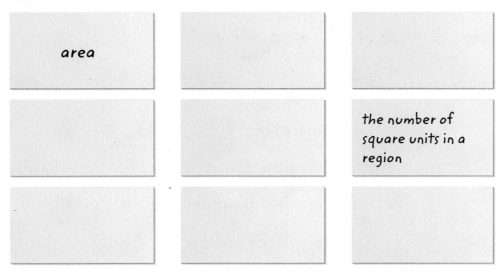

area

the number of square units in a region

▶ Math Journal [INDIVIDUALS]

As you learn new words, write them in your Math Journal. Write the definition of the word and include a sketch or an example. As you learn new information about the word, add notes to your definition.

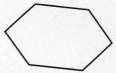
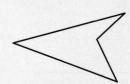

polygon: a closed plane figure with sides made of straight line segments.

In concave polygons, there exists a line segment with endpoints inside the polygon and a point on the line segment that is outside the polygon.

Vocabulary Activities (continued)

▶ What's the Word? PAIRS

Work together to make a poster or bulletin board display of
the words in a unit. Write definitions on a set of index cards.
Mix up the cards. Work with a partner, choosing a definition
from the index cards. Have your partner point to the word
on the poster and name the matching math vocabulary word.
Switch roles and try the activity again.

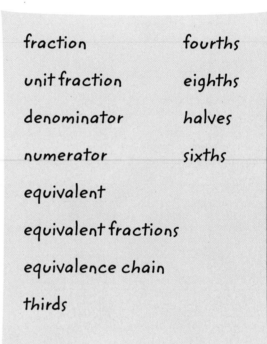

fraction   fourths

unit fraction   eighths

denominator   halves

numerator   sixths

equivalent

equivalent fractions

equivalence chain

thirds

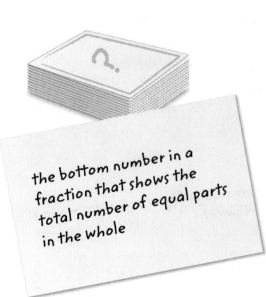

the bottom number in a
fraction that shows the
total number of equal parts
in the whole

Glossary

addend One of two or more numbers to be added together to find a sum.

Example: $8 + 4 = 12$

    addend   addend   sum

addition A mathematical operation that combines two or more numbers.

Example: $23 + 52 = 75$

    addend   addend   sum

adjacent (sides) Two sides of a figure that meet at a point.

Example: Sides a and b are adjacent.

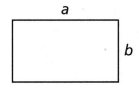

A.M. The time period between midnight and noon.

analog clock A clock with a face and hands.

angle A figure formed by two rays or two line segments that meet at an endpoint.

area The total number of square units that cover a figure.

Example: The area of the rectangle is 6 square units.

array An arrangement of objects, pictures, or numbers in columns and rows.

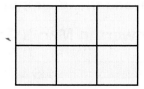

Associative Property of Addition (Grouping Property of Addition)

The property which states that changing the way in which addends are grouped does not change the sum.

Example: $(2 + 3) + 1 = 2 + (3 + 1)$

$$5 + 1 = 2 + 4$$

$$6 = 6$$

Associative Property of Multiplication (Grouping Property of Multiplication)

The property which states that changing the way in which factors are grouped does not change the product.

Example: $(2 \times 3) \times 4 = 2 \times (3 \times 4)$

$$6 \times 4 = 2 \times 12$$

$$24 = 24$$

Glossary (continued)

axis (plural: **axes**) A reference line for a graph. A graph has 2 axes; one is horizontal and the other is vertical.

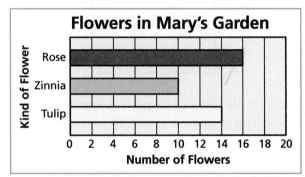

Flowers in Mary's Garden

B

bar graph A graph that uses bars to show data. The bars may be horizontal, as in the graph above, or vertical, as in the graph below.

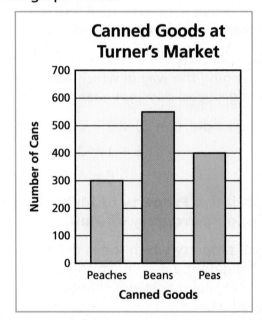

Canned Goods at Turner's Market

C

capacity The amount a container can hold.

centimeter (cm) A metric unit used to measure length.

100 centimeters = 1 meter

---

column A part of a table or array that contains items arranged vertically.

Commutative Property of Addition (Order Property of Addition) The property which states that changing the order of addends does not change the sum.

Example: 3 + 7 = 7 + 3

10 = 10

Commutative Property of Multiplication (Order Property of Multiplication) The property which states that changing the order of factors does not change the product.

Example: 5 × 4 = 4 × 5

20 = 20

comparison bars Bars that represent the greater amount, lesser amount, and difference in a comparison problem.

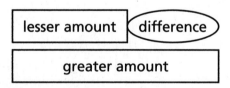

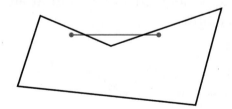

concave A polygon for which you can connect two points inside the polygon with a segment that passes outside the polygon.

convex A polygon is convex if all of its diagonals are inside it.

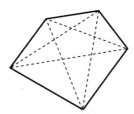

cup (c) A customary unit of measure used to measure capacity.

1 cup = 8 fluid ounces
2 cups = 1 pint
4 cups = 1 quart
16 cups = 1 gallon

D

data Pieces of information.

decagon A polygon with 10 sides.

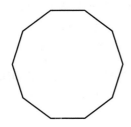

decimeter (dm) A metric unit used to measure length

1 decimeter = 10 centimeters

denominator The bottom number in a fraction that shows the total number of equal parts in the whole.

Example: $\frac{1}{3}$ ←——— denominator

diagonal A line segment that connects two corners of a figure and is not a side of the figure.

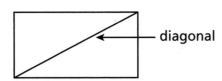
diagonal

difference The result of subtraction or of comparing.

digit Any of the symbols 0, 1, 2, 3, 4, 5, 6, 7, 8, 9.

digital clock A clock that displays the hour and minutes with numbers.

Distributive property You can multiply a sum by a number, or multiply each addend by the number and add the products; the result is the same.

Example:

$$3 \times (2 + 4) = (3 \times 2) + (3 \times 4)$$
$$3 \times 6 = 6 + 12$$
$$18 = 18$$

dividend The number that is divided in division.

Examples:

$$12 \div 3 = 4 \qquad 3\overline{)12}^{\,4}$$

dividend   dividend

division The mathematical operation that separates an amount into smaller equal groups to find the number of groups or the number in each group.

Example: 12 ÷ 3 = 4 is a division number sentence.

divisor The number that you divide by in division.

Example: $12 \div 3 = 4 \qquad 3\overline{)12}^{\,4}$

divisor   divisor

Glossary (continued)

elapsed time The time that passes between the beginning and the end of an activity.

endpoint The point at either end of a line segment or the beginning point of a ray.

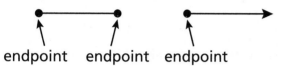

endpoint   endpoint   endpoint

equation A mathematical sentence with an equals sign.

Examples: 11 + 22 = 33
75 − 25 = 50

equivalent Equal, or naming the same amount.

equivalent fractions Fractions that name the same amount.

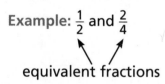

Example: $\frac{1}{2}$ and $\frac{2}{4}$

equivalent fractions

estimate About how many or about how much.

even number A whole number that is a multiple of 2. The ones digit in an even number is 0, 2, 4, 6, or 8.

expanded form A number written to show the value of each of its digits.

Examples:
347 = 300 + 40 + 7
347 = 3 hundreds + 4 tens + 7 ones

expression A combination of numbers, variables, and/or operation signs. An expression does not have an equals sign.

Examples: 4 + 7 $a − 3$

F

factors Numbers that are multiplied to give a product.

Example: 4 × 5 = 20

factor   factor   product

fluid ounce (fl oz) A unit of liquid volume in the customary system that equals $\frac{1}{8}$ cup or 2 tablespoons.

foot (ft) A customary unit used to measure length.

1 foot = 12 inches

fraction A number that names part of a whole or part of a set.

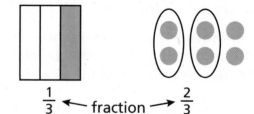

$\frac{1}{3}$ ← fraction → $\frac{2}{3}$

© Houghton Mifflin Harcourt Publishing Company

frequency table A table that shows how many times each event, item, or category occurs.

Frequency Table	
Age	**Tally**
7	1
8	3
9	5
10	4
11	2

function table A table of ordered pairs that shows a function.

For every input number, there is only one possible output number.

Rule: add 2	
Input	**Output**
1	3
2	4
3	5
4	6

G

gallon (gal) A customary unit used to measure capacity.

1 gallon = 4 quarts = 8 pints = 16 cups

gram (g) A metric unit of mass. One paper clip has a mass of about 1 gram.

1,000 grams = 1 kilogram

greater than (>) A symbol used to compare two numbers.

Example: 6 > 5
6 *is greater than* 5.

group To combine numbers to form new tens, hundreds, thousands, and so on.

H

height A vertical distance, or how tall something is.

hexagon A polygon with six sides.

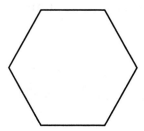

horizontal Extending in two directions, left and right.

horizontal bar graph A bar graph with horizontal bars.

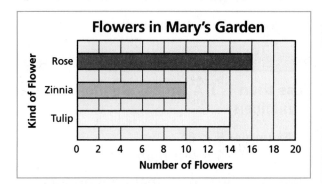

Identity Property of Addition If 0 is added to a number, the sum equals that number.

Example: 3 + 0 = 3

Identity Property of Multiplication The product of 1 and any number equals that number.

Example: 10 × 1 = 10

Glossary (continued)

improper fraction A fraction in which the numerator is equal to or is greater than the denominator. Improper fractions are equal to or greater than 1. $\frac{5}{5}$ and $\frac{8}{3}$ are improper fractions.

inch (in.) A customary unit used to measure length.

12 inches = 1 foot

K

key A part of a map, graph, or chart that explains what symbols mean.

kilogram (kg) A metric unit of mass.

1 kilogram = 1,000 grams

kilometer (km) A metric unit of length.

1 kilometer = 1,000 meters

L

less than (<) A symbol used to compare numbers.

Example: 5 < 6
          5 *is less than* 6.

line A straight path that goes on forever in opposite directions.

line plot A diagram that shows frequency of data on a number line. Also called a *dot plot*.

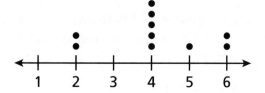

line segment A part of a line. A line segment has two endpoints.

●───────────●

liquid volume A measure of how much a container can hold. Also called *capacity*.

liter (L) A metric unit used to measure capacity.

1 liter = 1,000 milliliters

M

mass The amount of matter in an object.

mental math A way to solve problems without using pencil and paper or a calculator.

meter (m) A metric unit used to measure length.

1 meter = 100 centimeters

method A procedure, or way, of doing something.

mile (mi) A customary unit of length.

1 mile = 5,280 feet

milliliter (mL) A metric unit used to measure capacity.

1,000 milliliters = 1 liter

mixed number A whole number and a fraction.

$1\frac{3}{4}$ is a mixed number.

multiple A number that is the product of the given number and any whole number.

© Houghton Mifflin Harcourt Publishing Company

multiplication A mathematical operation that combines equal groups.

Example: 4 × 3 = 12

factor   factor   product

3 + 3 + 3 + 3 = 12

4 times

N
---

number line A line on which numbers are assigned to lengths.

numerator The top number in a fraction that shows the number of equal parts counted.

Example: $\frac{1}{3}$ ←— numerator

O
---

octagon A polygon with eight sides.

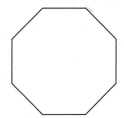

odd number A whole number that is not a multiple of 2. The ones digit in an odd number is 1, 3, 5, 7, or 9.

opposite sides Sides of a polygon that are across from each other; they do not meet at a point.

Example: Sides *a* and *c* are opposite.

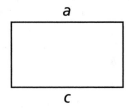

a

c

Order of operations A set of rules that state the order in which the operations in an expression should be done.

STEP 1: Perform operations inside parentheses first.

STEP 2: Multiply and divide from left to right.

STEP 3: Add and subtract from left to right.

ounce (oz) A customary unit used to measure weight.

16 ounces = 1 pound

P
---

parallel lines Two lines that are the same distance apart.

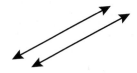

parallelogram A quadrilateral with both pairs of opposite sides parallel.

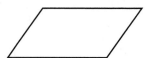

pentagon A polygon with five sides.

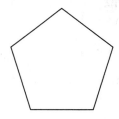

Glossary (continued)

perimeter The distance around a figure.

Example:

Perimeter = 3 cm + 5 cm + 3 cm + 5 cm = 16 cm

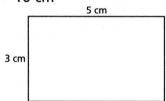

pictograph A graph that uses pictures or symbols to represent data.

Favorite Ice Cream Flavors

Peanut Butter Crunch	🍦 🍦
Cherry Vanilla	🍦 🍦 🍦
Chocolate	🍦 🍦 🍦 🍦

Each 🍦 stands for 4 votes.

pint (pt) A customary unit used to measure capacity.

1 pint = 2 cups

place value The value assigned to the place that a digit occupies in a number.

9   6   2

hundreds   tens   ones

place value drawing A drawing that represents a number. Hundreds are represented by boxes, tens by vertical lines, and ones by small circles.

962 (drawing of boxes, lines, and circles)

P.M. The time period between noon and midnight.

polygon A closed plane figure with sides made up of straight line segments.

pound (lb) A customary unit used to measure weight.

1 pound = 16 ounces

product The answer when you multiply numbers.

Example: 4 × 7 = 28

factor   factor   product

proof drawing A drawing used to show that an answer is correct.

$$\begin{array}{r} 249 \\ + 386 \\ \hline 11 \\ 635 \end{array}$$

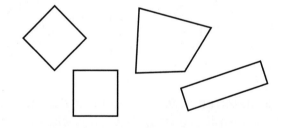

Q

quadrilateral A polygon with four sides.

quart (qt) A customary unit used to measure capacity.

1 quart = 4 cups

quotient The answer when you divide numbers.

Examples:

35 ÷ 7 = 5

quotient

5 ← quotient
7)35

© Houghton Mifflin Harcourt Publishing Company

R

ray A part of a line that has one endpoint and goes on forever in one direction.

rectangle A parallelogram that has 4 right angles.

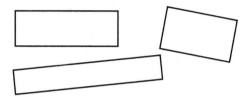

rhombus A parallelogram with congruent sides.

right angle An angle that measures 90°.

round To find about how many or how much by expressing a number to the nearest ten, hundred, thousand, and so on.

row A part of a table or array that contains items arranged horizontally.

S

scale An arrangement of numbers in order with equal intervals.

side (of a figure) One of the line segments that make up a polygon.

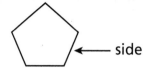
side

simplify To write an equivalent fraction with a smaller numerator and denominator.

situation equation An equation that shows the action or the relationship in a problem.

Example: $35 + n = 40$

solution equation An equation that shows the operation to perform in order to solve the problem.

Example: $n = 40 - 35$

square A rectangle with four sides of the same length.

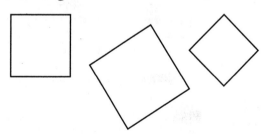

square number The product of a whole number and itself.

Example: $4 \times 4 = 16$

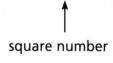
square number

square unit A unit of area equal to the area of a square with one-unit sides.

standard form The name of a number written using digits.

Example: 1,829

subtract To find the difference of two numbers.

Example: $18 - 11 = 7$

subtraction A mathematical operation on two numbers that gives the difference.

Example: $43 - 40 = 3$

sum The answer when adding two or more addends.

Example: $37 + 52 = 89$

addend   addend   sum

T

table An easy-to-read arrangement of data, usually in rows and columns.

Favorite Team Sport	
Sport	Number of Students
Baseball	35
Soccer	60
Basketball	40

tally marks Short line segments drawn in groups of 5. Each mark, including the slanted mark, stands for 1 unit.

‖‖‖ ‖‖‖ ‖‖‖ means 13
5   5   3

total The answer when adding two or more addends. The sum of two or more numbers.

Example: $672 + 228 = 900$

addend   addend   total
                           sum

trapezoid A quadrilateral with exactly one pair of parallel sides.

triangle A polygon with three sides.

U

ungroup To open up 1 in a given place to make 10 of the next smaller place value in order to subtract.

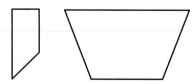

unit fraction A fraction whose numerator is 1. It shows one equal part of a whole.

Example: $\frac{1}{4}$

unit square A square whose area is 1 square unit.

V

variable A letter or symbol used to represent an unknown number in an algebraic expression or equation.

Example: $2 + n$

      n is a variable.

Venn diagram A diagram that uses circles to show the relationship among sets of objects.

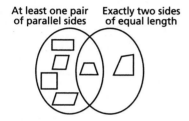

At least one pair of parallel sides   Exactly two sides of equal length

vertex A point where sides, rays, or edges meet.

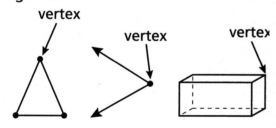

vertex   vertex   vertex

vertical Extending in two directions, up and down.

vertical bar graph A bar graph with vertical bars.

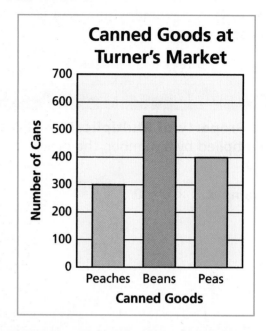

W

weight The measure of how heavy something is.

word form A name of a number written using words instead of digits.

Example: Nine hundred eighty-four

Glossary (continued)

Y

yard (yd) A customary unit used to measure length.

1 yard = 3 feet = 36 inches

Z

Zero Property of Multiplication If 0 is multiplied by a number, the product is 0.

Example: $3 \times 0 = 0$

Multiplication Table and Scrambled Tables (Volume 2)

E

×	4	2	5	1	3	8	10	7	9	6
4	16	8	20	4	12	32	40	28	36	24
1	4	2	5	1	3	8	10	7	9	6
2	8	4	10	2	6	16	20	14	18	12
5	20	10	25	5	15	40	50	35	45	30
3	12	6	15	3	9	24	30	21	27	18
9	36	18	45	9	27	72	90	63	81	54
6	24	12	30	6	18	48	60	42	54	36
10	40	20	50	10	30	80	100	70	90	60
7	28	14	35	7	21	56	70	49	63	42
8	32	16	40	8	24	64	80	56	72	48

F

×	9	8	6	7	4	6	8	7	4	9
2	18	16	12	14	8	12	16	14	8	18
3	27	24	18	21	12	18	24	21	12	27
5	45	40	30	35	20	30	40	35	20	45
3	27	24	18	21	12	18	24	21	12	27
5	45	40	30	35	20	30	40	35	20	45
9	81	72	54	63	36	54	72	63	36	81
7	63	56	42	49	28	42	56	49	28	63
6	54	48	36	42	24	36	48	42	24	54
8	72	64	48	56	32	48	64	56	32	72
4	36	32	24	28	16	24	32	28	16	36

G

×	7	6	8	7	8	6	8	7	6	8
5	35	30	40	35	40	30	40	35	30	40
4	28	24	32	28	32	24	32	28	24	32
3	21	18	24	21	24	18	24	21	18	24
2	14	12	16	14	16	12	16	14	12	16
8	56	48	64	56	64	48	64	56	48	64
9	63	54	72	63	72	54	72	63	54	72
7	49	42	56	49	56	42	56	49	42	56
6	42	36	48	42	48	36	48	42	36	48
8	56	48	64	56	64	48	64	56	48	64
6	42	36	48	42	48	36	48	42	36	48

H

×	4	6	7	8	9	6	9	8	7	4
4	16	24	28	32	36	24	36	32	28	16
6	24	36	42	48	54	36	54	48	42	24
7	28	42	49	56	63	42	63	56	49	28
8	32	48	56	64	72	48	72	64	56	32
9	36	54	63	72	81	54	81	72	63	36
8	32	48	56	64	72	48	72	64	56	32
9	36	54	63	72	81	54	81	72	63	36
4	16	24	28	32	36	24	36	32	28	16
7	28	42	49	56	63	42	63	56	49	28
6	24	36	42	48	54	36	54	48	42	24